HILLS OF HOPE

The Autobiography
of
Jama Matakata

Nutrend Productions

Published by: Nutrend Productions, 14 Killarney Terrace
                 Pietermaritzburg, 3201

First published 2004

ISBN 0-9584614-7-3

Acknowledgement: The publisher would like to acknowledge, with thanks, Die Burger for
providing the cover photograph.

Layout and Design: Rockbottom (033) 3961378
Cover Design: Afrimage Communications
Cover Photograph: Die Burger

Printed by Intrepid Printers, Pietermaritzburg
7203

Contents

iv

Acknowledgements

This book owes its existence to a number of people:

Oliver Reginald Tambo, my role model and source of inspiration; Nelson Mandela, whom I have always admired and respected; Mr. Alpheus Ndlovu, the late High Commissioner of South Africa in Lesotho and the honourable Minister of Home Affairs for Lesotho, Mr. Thabane, who shared their experiences with me and fuelled my motivation to write.

Ingunn Sofie Aursnes of Norway, who encouraged me to write about my experiences.

Ex-political prisoners, former exiles and colleagues who kept reminding me that this exercise was long overdue.

The South Africans who created a space for me in the history of my country and the people of Paarl who kept me in their prayers and high esteem.

Autshumatu Investments (Pty) Ltd for helping me regain my dignity.

Fallen fighters and their families whose precious lives were such meaningful contributions.

...*HILLS OF HOPE* is for all of you.

Dedication

I dedicate this book to my wife, Asanda; my children, Thandolwethu and Ako; my father and mother; my brothers and sisters - who have always supported me; and the National Baptist Church who helped shape me into the person I am today.

HILLS OF HOPE is also, in itself, a dedication to those comrades who died in the course of the struggle. It is a tribute to the unsung heroes and heroines who rewrote history by giving their lives for the cause. They have never been hailed and recognized as such in our history books.

Thanks

Thank you Asanda, my beloved wife. Without your motivation and support, this book would never have been possible. You were wonderful – typing and editing my manuscripts over and over again. The time you spent on my project was truly incredible and very much appreciated.

My sincere thanks go to Phindi and Sthembi Dlamini of Nutrend Productions for their tremendous assistance in realizing my dream and to Cherry Stoltz for editing my manuscript and creating the maps with such diligence. Her input enlightened and empowered me in my desire to help others.

I am extremely appreciative of the support of the International Defence and Aid Fund; Amnesty International; International Red Cross; Anti-Apartheid Movement; Anthea Sheldon; Susan Bancomile Cele; Mongezi Sotheni; Mlungisi Matsam; Claire Wright; Africa Hlapo; Vuyokazi Mbulawa; Asanda Bangani; Cecil Esau; Vuyiswa Moko; Zola Williams; Mnini Matakata; James Gibson; Andrew Ramokopelo; Erica Avril Mc Carthy; Patrick Mangashe and Janine Da Rebeira.

Special thanks to the African National Congress for contributing to my political upbringing.
And to those whom I may have forgotten, I shall forever be in your debt.

Preface

There is a great deal of political responsibility to be carried out by men and women who have the future of our country at heart. Post-Apartheid South Africa still faces a huge eco-political backlog that needs to be adequately addressed. Furthermore, leaving the country's administration in the hands of the very same apartheid-era operators and their compromised agents within the liberation movement – for the sake of propagating reconciliation - creates conditions that, in the future, may greatly compromise our political gains and achievements.

Today, South Africans speak with a voice that almost ignores the past - as if it simply did not exist. The need to reflect our past is a necessity in terms of those who offered their lives and were subjected to endless tortures in apartheid detention centres, those whose lives were wasted in apartheid prisons and the oppressed South Africans who experienced misery and mental pain. Last, but not least, we need to express our history in terms of the noble ideals we fought for, ideals that kept us committed to end apartheid and its associated evils, as well as the class conflict beyond apartheid.

This book records the experiences of a group of young anti-apartheid activists in their struggle to create a new social order that would be of benefit to all who live in South Africa. Though many died in their quest for a better future, the experiences of those who survived cemented them into one vast family, committed to the defence and development of their motherland. The recording and reflection of our past is of great necessity in ensuring that our history will neither be lost nor distorted.

We owe a great amount of gratitude to all the sons and daughters mentioned in this book and to fellow cadres who fought and stood alongside us to the very last. Let us never forget ...

By Colonel Patrick Ricketts

Introduction

This book is my attempt to inform people about the events and conditions that some of us found ourselves in. It is also my humble contribution to those who have always supported, protected and prayed for me during the years of struggle. It seeks to bestow honour, integrity and respect to the men and women who selflessly contributed their lives to make me – a proud product of the people's struggle in South Africa. Many of them are mentioned in my story. *HILLS OF HOPE* is meant to be a cultural recording of a certain part of history aimed at encouraging our generation and generations to come, urging them to leave no stone unturned in ensuring that these individuals, groups, organizations and institutions are remembered forever. Memories are mirrors that reflect both painful and joyful experiences. No matter how bitter, they are part of our history and we must take pride in them and our achievements as collective groups and individuals. No one is more, or less, important in terms of sacrifices made to attain liberation.

I have journeyed throughout the country and observed that we deny South Africans, and the world at large, stories about ordinary people. I have witnessed situations where men struggled to write the obituaries of fallen comrades due to lack of documented information. Therefore as an activist, former exile, ex-combatant and ex-political prisoner, I find it necessary to share some of our experiences and acknowledge the efforts of unsung martyrs. In places like Robben Island and the military camps, ordinary people sacrificed their youth for the cause. Writing this story is a gift no one can take from me - and a mark that cannot be erased. It is the story of what I am today and where I come from and is also one of my proudest achievements.

Great leaders in our time will no doubt agree that the need for ordinary foot soldiers to record their experiences is long overdue. This is something we need to promote as a nation. Our older generation told the story from their perspective, but little has been recorded by the youth of our country. There are so many helpless, hopeless and dejected South Africans whom I know can identify with aspects of this book. I hope to inspire comrades of my own generation – those who were activists, went into exile, or were sent to prison for their political beliefs – to do the same.

In a few places, only the person's first or last name is mentioned, either to protect their identity or due to difficulties in establishing their full names. UMkhonto weSizwe *noms de guerre* are either written in brackets or within single inverted commas.

MAP OF SOUTHERN AFRICA

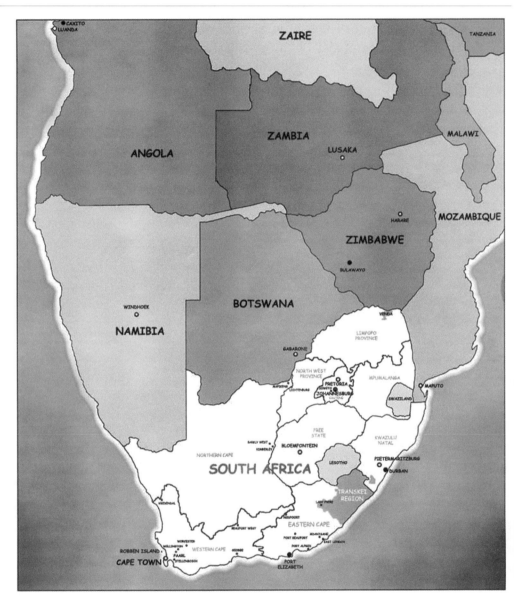

CHAPTER 1

Early Days

Born on the 21st of December in 1961, I was the fifth of nine children born to Oliver and Nobengazi Matakata, raised in a modest, humble home at Paarl – in an area then called Langabuya. My father was born at Lady Frere and my mother at Noupoort, both places being in the Eastern Cape. He is a stubborn man whereas she is gentle and humble, yet both share a great sense of humour.

Paarl is situated 52 km from Cape Town and popularly known as the place where Nelson Mandela spent his last years of incarceration at Victor Verster Prison. The town is also famous for its wineries and the '*Afrikaans Taal* (Language) *Monument*'. In 1975, Afrikaans celebrated its centenary as a language. Millions of rands were spent on the erection of a monument, which meant more poverty for disadvantaged communities.

My birthplace is rich in both Afrikaner and Black resistance history. It is where many political activities took place, ranging from trade unionism to student politics and the liberation struggle. A number of people were killed there during the Poqo uprisings of the 1960's as a result of pass law protests. Numerous people died during feuds between the United Democratic Front (UDF) and the Azanian Peoples Organization (AZAPO) in 1985. I am of the generation that helped to change visible Pan Africanist Congress (PAC) sentiments in Paarl to those of the African National Congress (ANC) during the 1980s.

For many years, my parents temporarily housed other families in informal houses built in our backyard. These people arrived from the Eastern Cape and moved out as soon as they found permanent accommodation. As one family left, the next moved in. This practice was not unusual. Many other householders in our area did the same thing. Hospitality was never seen as an inconvenience but a gift to others in need. Occasionally, itinerant families overflowed into our house and, as children, my siblings and I often slept on the floor. At times, we shared the little food we had with families who had none.

On certain Sundays, a family friend from Gugulethu Township came to lunch. Mlungisi Kwini had an incredible appetite and my parents knew that his plate always had to be filled to the brim and include meat. I do not remember him ever leaving a scrap of food.

After school on weekdays I supplemented our family income by selling plastic buckets. One of my neighbours, Dambile Kweleta, bought them from Textile Factory and employed a few younger children as junior salesmen. He paid fifty cents for each bucket sold. Dambile's brother, Norman, was more or less my age so we joined forces, selling to the hostel dwellers. They brewed homemade beer in the buckets. It was called 'Umqombothi' or 'Amarewu' – a concoction prepared from soft maize porridge and fermented into a liquid. On weekends, I sometimes helped Norman's brother, Mancedo 'Max' Kweleta, to collect outstanding debts from clients. Max worked for Dan Hands furniture shop and used the company van. He always paid me something afterwards, which I immediately gave to my mother.

Alcohol abuse was rife in the townships, particularly among hostel dwellers. After work, they invariably headed straight for the municipal beer hall. On weekends, I watched inebriated old people struggling to walk home. Drunks lay in the street, unable to remember their names. It was not a pretty sight. As children, we helped many of them to their feet and tried to make sense out of their mumblings. A few of the children teased them and were insulted and chased away for their insolence.

Beer halls were always filled to maximum capacity. The homebrew on sale was far more potent and acidic than traditional beer, leaving holes in the floor where drops had fallen.

I have never personally tasted alcohol but soon observed how it destroyed my people. Alcohol abuse almost ruined my family during those early years. When he drank, my father physically abused my mother. At times, she drank as well and would sometimes run away with us to seek refuge with a relative. It was a painful experience. We could do nothing to stop it. I knew my mother was sad and I found the whole situation totally confusing until the wonderful day that both of them became committed Christians and stopped drinking.

My education started in 1969 when I was eight years old but I found school a subtle form of torture. It was even worse during winter months when freezing weather deposited frost on the grass. I would shiver uncontrollably, trying to hold a wood-framed slate in half-frozen arms; barefoot and clad in nothing more than a pair of grey shorts and a blue shirt. Few of us had shoes because our parents could not afford them. I rubbed Vaseline onto the exposed parts of my body, firmly believing that it protected me from the severe cold, but the exercise was futile. On rainy days, I ran as fast as I could to avoid getting wet. Of course that did not work either but I was too young to understand at the time, convinced that the rain could not possibly catch up with me. Occasionally, I spent the entire day at school in wet clothes. Being sent home to change was a luxury, dispensed at a teacher's discretion.

Jama's first school – 1969.

I tried to avoid going to school but my mother always found out and spanked me with one of her slippers. This punishment was invariably administered in public, on the way to school, and was a tremendous humiliation. She had never been to school herself but fully understood the importance of an education. Like any good parent, my mother did not want her children to suffer the same disadvantages as she had. She must have been very disappointed when I failed the first grade and had to repeat it the following year.

There were no chairs in our classroom. We knelt on the cement floor to write, governed by the fear of making a mistake – and knowing the consequences if we did. Teachers tolerated no mistakes and were very harsh in those days. Our school consisted of nothing more than one small building opposite Mbekweni Post Office. We shared the building with a dairy but later moved into the community hall. Different classes occupied the same open space, divided by imaginary boundaries. While we were busy with our lessons, other class activities made it difficult to concentrate and, at times, we found ourselves focusing on the things they were doing - particularly if they were more interesting. Certain teachers became more intolerant as we grew older, resulting in a considerable number of children leaving school due to corporal punishment. In my opinion, physical punishment did far more harm than good to African children and, inadvertently, our country. My cousin walked out of class the day a teacher punished her for not knowing the correct answer to a question and she did not return for the rest of that year. We were even punished for our inability to recite 'Die Stem van Suid Afrika' – the national anthem at that time. Fortunately, a few teachers were humanitarians who treated us like their own children.

During my primary school years, particularly when I progressed to higher levels, an awareness of huge discrepancies regarding unequal treatment of whites and blacks became clear. White schools were well maintained, well constructed and had better facilities. In my ignorance, I wanted to be 'a white kid' - based on the preferential treatment I perceived them to be given. I honestly believed that all white people were rich, especially when trucks from Jones and Langeberg – the canning factories - brought excess fruit to Mbekweni. They dumped the fruit in an open field behind the Dutch Reformed Church, where annual IsiXhosa and SeSotho cultural activities were held. To my juvenile mind this meant that whites had so much that they could afford to give it away.

One of my boyhood friends, Maboy Ndevu, kept us out of mischief by telling his wonderful stories. Every day after school, I visited Maboy at his home. He was able to create fiction as though it were real. Sometimes, he narrated one of James Hadley Chase's books, adding his own exciting embellishments as he went along. Maboy's talent became even clearer when he wrote and directed a play in 1982 with the title *'CRY NO MORE',* about a youngster whose parents were oppressed. The youngster stopped weeping over his situation and left to join the exiled liberation army instead.

I also grew up with the very talented and innovative Solomzi Bisholo – one of the actors in Maboy's play. He eventually became a cast member in the famous play *'ASINIMALI',* written and directed by Mbongeni Ngema - depicting a political campaign championed by Msizi Dube, an activist in protest against the payment of services to municipalities. The play was staged nationally and internationally.

Rugby and Soccer played a big part in my life too. Our coach, Phumendlini Kalase, was very strict and always stressed the importance of discipline and taking sport seriously. Much as we enjoyed playing, the meal his wife prepared afterwards was definitely an added incentive. I only started applying myself to serious study from Grade 8. Prior to that, karate and games were far more appealing.

In 1973, I passed Grade 3 at Langabuya Primary and then went to Mbekweni Higher Primary. After completing my higher primary education at Mbekweni, I moved over to Simon Hebe Junior Secondary school where I completed Grades 8, 9 and 10. At Simon Hebe, we often held debates on various political and social matters. I always looked forward to these discussions. In rural and semi-rural areas like Paarl, many injustices took place. People were constantly dehumanized and denied their rights. Blacks had to carry a *dompas* (as identity documents were known) and were constantly harassed. They were refused permission to be in urban areas because they "belonged in their homeland". On farms, at work, in health institutions – in fact everywhere – one would witness these scenes. Conditions of employment were shocking. In some cases, people received cheap wine as compensation for hard labour.

At times, my family went without food and was forced to ask the neighbours for help. I witnessed the anger of my people. I felt the frustration of parents who wanted to give their children an education but could not afford to do so. I tasted bitterness and suffering working on wine farms as a casual labourer from thirteen to eighteen years of age, bringing home meagre wages handed out by the *oubaas*. The term, an Afrikaans form of address meaning 'old master', was used to show respect to white employers. Their children had to be addressed as *kleinbaas* ('young master') – irrespective of age.

One Friday I overslept, missing the truck that took us to work on the wine farm. I was paid no salary the following week and felt cheated because my family desperately needed the money. My cousin spoke on my behalf. Not being fluent in Afrikaans, I could not do so for myself.

At one stage, I worked at Langeberg Food and Canning Factory during the December school holidays, breaking down a section of reinforced concrete with a jackhammer. It was a dreadful experience. During the night, my body shook uncontrollably as if I were suffering from epilepsy - but I had to help my family to survive. The money would be used to send us to school.

Unless one has no pride at all, one cannot simply sit back and take this sort of abuse. Illiteracy, poverty, unemployment and housing shortages are still some of the biggest problems facing black people.

CHAPTER 2

My Introduction to the World of Politics

Many things contributed to my involvement in politics. As a child, my father told me about apartheid and how negatively it affected our country. Later on, I understood how the apartheid system oppressed our people and why they struggled for equality. Initially, my political education came from listening to cassette tapes of Oliver Tambo's speeches and reading banned ANC material – pamphlets and the Mayibuye Publications. Occasionally, I listened to Radio Freedom. All this input helped to shape me and instil a sense of personal obligation. I remember Tambo's 68th ANC Anniversary speech on January the 8th 1980; "Cemeteries are full of black infants – in this year of the child?" He was angry. Children should be loved and cared for, not harmed. He added, "We do not fight to reform apartheid, but to abolish it in its entirety." I was intensely moved by his speech, hated the white regime and felt a great sense of patriotism. I sensed a deep need to play a part in ending white minority rule and understood even better what the ANC stood for. It made me angry to realize that our people were killed simply for standing up for their rights.

I loved reggae music too and listened with my friends. Bob Marley, Rodney Winston and Peter Tosh all reminded us that we were oppressed and should fight for our freedom. These, and many other reasons, made me realize that it was not enough to sit and wait for things to change – I had to help bring about the change.

In September of 1977, Simon Hebe School participated in a tour organized by Mbekweni Higher Primary during the September school holidays. We drove in two buses (one for boys and the other for girls), leaving Paarl in the late afternoon and arriving at Oudtshoorn to watch a fundraising function where pupils providing short plays and choral music. We slept over that night and went on to the Eastern Cape the following morning, stopping at the beach in Port Elizabeth along the way. This was very exciting. The boys immediately went for a swim. Most of the girls and a few prefects stayed on the buses.

Our teachers bought a sheep for the evening meal. They needed assistance with the slaughtering but we were still swimming. When we arrived back from the beach, everything was already prepared. Teachers ordered us to wait in the bus while everyone else ate. Afterwards, they brought us very small pieces of sheep intestines and tripe. Everyone knew it was a form of punishment. Not at all satisfied with the state of affairs, we climbed off the bus and gathered outside. Older boys complained about the unfair practice and decided to boycott the tour, telling the teachers that they had no intention of staying with the tour unless they were given proper food – or a refund.

It was terribly cold. Some of us wore nothing more than the underwear we had swam in. As the wind intensified, the younger boys (myself included) gradually withdrew and returned to the bus with the excuse that we had to fetch warmer clothing. The older boys made us promise to return but we were far too cold and hungry, and afraid of being left behind. Initially a large group, eventually only seventeen boys remained outside, standing firmly by their decision. Teachers made several futile attempts to compromise and then decided to leave them behind. This decision brought tears to many of us, especially the girls. The abandoned boys were reported to the nearest police station for their safety and protection before our buses made their way to Alice near Fort Beaufort. Understandably, the atmosphere was somewhat tense and no one enjoyed the tour from that moment.

On the way back we stopped at Worcester to have a *braai* in the *veld*.

Some of the boys prepared the barbeque and others organized a quick meeting to discuss the plight of those who had been left behind. Our meeting was interrupted when the principal, Mr. Tsholoba, called us to eat so we left Worcester without finalizing matters.

As soon as we arrived at Mbekweni, we noticed policemen and vans all over the place. The seventeen students had managed to reach Paarl on their own and went to Mr. Simon Hebe, a school committee member, to demand their money back - which they never received. Earlier that day, parents requested permission to hold a meeting in order to discuss the problem. A number of student groups waited anxiously outside the community hall for the outcome. The students numbered more than the permitted amount and constituting an illegal gathering. At that time, an official act had been passed stating that any gathering of more than ten people discussing political matters, or having any political intentions, was regarded as illegal. Police ordered us to disperse but we ignored the warning. They fired teargas canisters and the situation grew increasingly chaotic. People ran in all directions, bumped into each other and were knocked down. The police chased us and managed to arrest some of the students who were later released. Eventually my uncle, Velile Mgwayi – a policeman at the time – took the seventeen boys to the police station but they were released later as well. As a youngster, I wanted to be a policeman. The power that my uncle's uniform afforded and the fear and respect people showed him had quite an impact on me, although I knew he was hated in some areas.

Sometime later a few of us assembled under a tree in an open field and agreed to support the seventeen students by boycotting classes. Additional grievances fuelled our determination, some of which were not directly related to the issue at hand. Certain students had paid for books and blazers but never received them. Oddly enough when Mr. Ndzuzo – a strict disciplinarian and member of the school committee – was called to speak to us, no one said a word at first.

He walked straight up to me as we were standing around outside the classrooms and asked what the problem was. Confused, I looked to the older boys for help but they whispered back, telling me to speak on their behalf. This put me in a 'Catch 22' situation because there was no way of appeasing my colleagues and Mr. Ndzuzo. It was a dreadful feeling.

Nevertheless, I dived in head first, mentioned that the students were unhappy about a number of things and promptly listed them. Excluding myself from the issues was a big mistake. My fellow students were not impressed and whispered again, reminding me to use the word 'us' instead of 'them'. Mr. Ndzuzo put his hand on my head as if we were father and child but I felt bad about letting the group down.

Parents and teachers made promises to address the grievances. We were ordered to return to classes and continue studying. To the best of my knowledge our grievances were never properly addressed. This incident changed my thinking and bred a firm determination to learn more about politics. Something needed to be done about the unfair treatment we received and to improve conditions at school.

CHAPTER 3

Congress of South African Students (COSAS)

Towards the end of 1979, Wantu Zenzile – a COSAS (Congress of South African Students) national organizer – and Patrick Ricketts who was instrumental in organizing the meeting, met with our student group in Paarl. Patrick is a tall, well–built coloured man and dedicated political activist. We held our first session in the bushes at a place called Anthony's Vlei in Wellington, where we discussed the formation of a branch in Paarl. It was pouring with rain so we sat inside a yellow truck belonging to Mr. Essop, raising our voices because of the noise. Rain dripped through holes in the truck but it was the safest venue we could find at the time.

Our second session took place at New Orleans Park and included Mthetheleli Titana, Ndodomzi Mkabile, Patrick Ricketts, Lloyd Fortuin, myself, and others. The purpose of this meeting was to share ideas on how we could best advance student politics. Mthetheleli was very intelligent and a talented sportsman with a wonderful sense of humour. One of the founder members of COSAS in Mbekweni, he had a strong character and an uncompromising love for the ANC and its liberation army – uMkhonto weSizwe (Spear of the nation). At school, he excelled in Mathematics and Physical Science. Lloyd was politically shrewd and totally committed in his attempts to recruit and influence students within the coloured community. Very alert and vigilant, he had managed to avoid detention by the police in most cases.

I became one of the founder members in Paarl – the first COSAS branch in the Western Cape at the time. The group voted Mthetheleli in as Chairperson and myself as Organizer. In the same year, Patrick recruited me into ANC underground structures and we began to build the organization, conducting most of our clandestine meetings under a tree in Mbekweni. We called the tree 'Worcester' – a random codename that enabled us to convey telephonic messages without giving away our position. It was distinctly possible that police might use bugging devices so we observed strict underground rules in most cases, never discussing our affairs over the telephone. We kept meeting points and agendas a secret, communicating with one another by means of a unique system of whistles.

Another student body was formed called 'The Committee of 81', consisting of 81 representatives in the Western Cape, mainly coloured students. The representatives came from secondary schools, technikons and universities but earned our disrespect by excluding African students. Coloured students were perceived to be only interested in coloured schools. Our concerns proved to be justified sometime later when they called off an organized strike, leaving African students to continue the boycott alone. The purpose of this strike was to abolish separate Bantu Education and demand equal education for all. The Bantu Education System compelled students and teachers to use Afrikaans as the language of instruction. Inferior syllabuses ensured school–leavers an inferior status in the work place and discouraged any creative thinking at all.

African schools organized themselves and formed a Committee chaired by Kente Mkalipa. Our group from Paarl were invited to join this 'Committee of Ten' in Gugulethu but we were unimpressed by the style and quality of leadership and their thinking differed dramatically from ours. Leaders were more concerned with individual image than the cause of those whom they served. This was distinctly contrary to our beliefs. We were particularly discouraged because committee members were either BCM (Black Consciousness Movement) or PAC (Pan African Congress) inclined. The BCM emerged in the 1970s under the leadership of Steve Biko, bringing pride and confidence to black people and stressing the importance of taking responsibility for one's own destiny. The PAC thought the ANC too accommodating, soft and liberal and broke away in 1959 because they did not agree with the freedom charter.

We decided to concentrate our efforts and fight the struggle in our hometown, making students aware of what was happening through discussion and pamphlet distribution. As part of the leadership structure in charge of directing massive bus and meat boycotts during 1980 and 1981, we gave instructions to the locals that no schools were to be burnt down and no human lives lost as a result of the actions. They followed our instructions to the letter. Unfortunately, the radical militants who preceded us were exposed to a different belief system and the trend was for students to burn down schools, demanding better facilities. Paarl suffered terribly in terms of the loss of human lives. This was a direct result of black on black violence instigated by the earlier regime. Today, Paarl still bleeds from the wounds their legacy left behind.

Other problems arose during the 1980 boycotts. At Simon Hebe, students targeted teachers whom they alleged were spies for the police. One of the teachers was Miss Stengana. Her hearing took place in the school library. Some of the students were demanding to have her killed for passing on information about student activities. I arrived to find Miss Stengana sobbing helplessly, desperately trying to defend herself. I personally intervened on her behalf, first asking why she was there. The crowd shouted that she was an informer but no one could produce any proof in support of the allegation, other than a few students who claimed to have seen her climbing out of a Mr. Mngqibisa's car. He was a Special Branch official who often gave lifts to people from town on his way to Mbekweni. I insisted on specifics. No one replied. Without further ado, I released Miss Stengana and told her to leave, sternly warning the students about sowing trouble and disrupting our unity. The relief in her eyes was unbelievable.

Right up until her death in a car accident, she worked tirelessly for the community and left behind a wonderful gift – Nomzamo Educare Crèche. Miss Stengana personally raised funds for building the crèche to educate pre–school children.

In other parts of South Africa, many people found themselves in the same predicament and were condemned to death on unsubstantiated allegations during the apartheid years. In spite of these dreadful events we continued to build COSAS. Everywhere we went words of encouragement came from a number of activists. During 1980, African students did not attend school for the entire year because of the boycott. My comrades and I visited students in Cape Town and in Worcester instead, gathering as much information as we could.

I was fortunate enough to be recruited as a volunteer by Miss Stengana, to teach Basic English and Numeracy to adults in Mbekweni. She was Principal of the Adult Education School. I conducted classes on a part time basis in the evenings and enjoyed teaching tremendously and, as a result, won the confidence of the elderly, particularly among hostel dwellers. Over weekends, a few of my students invited me for a meal. They treated me with great respect even though I was so young and still in Grade 10. In turn, I accorded them the same respect and saw myself as making a valuable contribution in boosting their confidence. Unfortunately, due to the school boycotts, I had to repeat tenth grade the following year.

All along, our main objective was to receive military training and obtain weapons for our fight against apartheid. Mthetheleli Titana, Xolile 'Joe' Tisana, Ndodomzi Mkabile and myself were the main forces behind student politics in Mbekweni. We got to know Liz Abrahams and Nomalizo Phike, both veterans of the women's league and trade unionism. They gave us some very good ideas and taught us more about the ANC.

Desperate to leave South Africa, we approached a man named John Phendlani and Willy Allah – both staunch ANC underground activists – and asked them to help us find suitable contacts but they refused. Joe, Mthetheleli, Ndodomzi, Michael Crail and I sat in the veld one day with an atlas, hoping to find a possible route to Botswana or Lesotho. Nothing came of it because none of us had a clue as to what these countries looked like in the first place. Ndodomzi and Joe were COSAS members from my township and we all shared the same dream – to liberate the oppressed masses of South Africa.

Yusuf Patel took us to Faldie Vahen's house where we remained underground, constantly looking for a way to leave the country. We were bitterly disappointed. The two men had connections in Libya but told us to finish our studies first. At the time Libya only assisted the PAC, not the ANC, so we were right back to square one. It seemed doubtful whether our attempts would ever yield any positive results so our morale was very low.

During the same period, the Security Branch harassed and detained Siphiwo Mthimkhulu of Port Elizabeth, another staunch COSAS member. Siphiwo vigorously campaigned against the apartheid regime from a student activist's perspective. After finding out that he was at Groote Schuur Hospital, my comrades and I went to visit him. When we arrived a white priest was there, speaking to him. Sure that this man's presence was nothing more than a police tactic to monitor Siphiwo's visitors and discussions we left soon after, having said very little. It was dreadful to see our comrade in such a poor physical state. The second time we went, Siphiwo's parents were there. His hair was falling out and he told us the security branch had poisoned him. Athough Siphiwo was in a lot of pain he managed to crack a few jokes, pretending to be Oliver Tambo (president of the ANC) whom he worshipped. His condition brought home the importance of leaving South Africa and continuing with our freedom struggle from a neighbouring country. I was very worried about being arrested and suffering the same torture.

Fort Hare University in the Transkei boycotted classes as well and, as a result, the university was closed, forcing students to return to their respective homes. Nelson Mandela studied at this institution as a young man.

Fort Hare students from the Western Cape requested us to give them a platform so they could explain the reasons behind the boycotts to the community. There were mixed reactions. Some of the local students felt it was opportunism while others welcomed the idea. We decided to give them the platform anyway, allowing them to address the entire community in Mbekweni Hall. They explained exactly what we stood for; the eradication of discrimination in schools, the abolishment of inferior Bantu Education and the provision of a better future for black students. It was a cause worth fighting for. Mrs. Nkala stood up and told the fully packed hall that she was giving her daughter Phumla over to the struggle – to participate in the fight for liberation with no resistance from the family, even if Phumla died in the process. Her message confirmed that we were engaged in a very serious matter. Phumla stood up and was a force to be reckoned with – dedicated and clear minded in what she wanted to achieve, brave, committed and uncompromising.

We called upon local students to help boycott the sale of red meat in support of Cape Town abattoir workers. The company was exploiting them and, by boycotting the abattoirs, they would suffer financially and be forced to accept their employees' demands; better working conditions and better wages. We met with the community at Simon Hebe Secondary School and requested their support. They promised to do so but, inevitably, a few continued to buy red meat covertly.

Bus drivers at City Tramways demanded better working conditions as well and called us to boycott the buses. We made sure that their call was heeded by appealing for the community not to use buses and not to go to work. The community also protested against increased bus fares. On June the 16th, we made a firm statement by staying away from work to commemorate and mourn the youth who were killed by the police on that day in 1976. This was a form of protest meant to register our point and create an economic dent. We distributed pamphlets on trains and at taxi ranks in Mbekweni and Paarl.

A number of people showed great resistance. One gentleman spoke up saying that we, the students, were misleading old people and that the day of mourning should be honoured by observing a moment of silence in the work place. He was opposed to any form of boycott and believed it was unwise to stay away because white employers could be merciless and victimize workers. He intended going to work irrespective of our decision. The boycott continued but we found out later that he had, in fact, stayed away.

Very early on the day, we set out to monitor train stations and bus terminals. Nzimeni Makhamba, an ANC die–hard, led the way. Commuters took their chances but turned back as soon as they saw us. Contract workers travelling in trucks were stopped, mainly hostel dwellers. We anticipated resistance from them but, to my surprise, most respected our request and instructed their drivers to return home. A few jumped out before they reached us. Some resorted to other means of transport.

While we were still continuing with the school boycott, Radi Ndevu, Lawrence Magogotya and Norman Kweleta went to work, contrary to what was agreed on. They were not convinced that the boycott would yield fruitful results. A decision was taken to look for them and bring them in front of the students to account for their actions. Being very close to these men, I was caught in an awkward situation. We had grown up together. Norman was my friend and neighbour. We went to Norman's parents where the students insisted that Mr. and Mrs. Kweleta hand their son over to rejoin us. He was not home. Behind me, someone in the crowd began throwing stones. I looked back into the darkness demanding to know who was responsible, as no instruction had been given to do so.

I felt really bad, knowing how the incident would strain neighbour relations. Our two families would be in conflict because of my involvement and I would be the first person targeted by the police because I lived next door. In addition, his family knew I had a huge influence over the students and probably felt I should have urged them to find an alternative course of action. Unfortunately it was too late. Everything happened very quickly. Norman's brother Max approached the mob and called out my name. The crowd booed and told him to leave. Max wanted to fetch Norman but was afraid he would be beaten up, until we promised not to harm him. Norman came to us the following day.

Lawrence and Radi were eventually captured in the township and brought to school to account for their actions but they drew knives, opened a way through the students, and fled. The situation returned to normal once they decided to join the boycott.

Not long afterwards, Officers Blankenberg and Daniels of the South African Police Security Branch arrested Ndodomzi Mkabile, Mthetheleli and Joe Titana, Kenny Jacobs, Albert Kulsen, Mpumi Peterson, Lloyd Fortuin, Van den Berg Pienaar, Gerald Andrews, Fatima and Malam Mehtar, Marlon Govender and myself for illegal gathering.

Malam and Fatima lived with their sister who was married to Dr. Jamie. He was not connected to COSAS in any way but sometimes assisted us with finance. On this particular occasion, a small group of students met in his garage to discuss politics and devise strategies for the boycott. During the meeting, we heard a knock at the door. Not expecting any trouble we opened up to find the police standing there. Mpumi, Lloyd and myself jumped through the window but I fell into the hands of officer Daniels. The thought of going to prison terrified me. What about my parents? What if I were tortured? Unfortunately it was Friday as well, which meant being kept in a holding cell for the weekend along with common criminals.

Criminals in the holding cell took Kenny's spectacles away but gave them back when he told them he could not see. Then they stripped Ndodomzi of his trousers and searched him, hoping to find something of value. They did not discover a thing. We were released out on bail on the Monday. As minors, Ndodomzi, Mthetheleli and I were given free bail and placed into the custody of our parents. Actually none of us were minors but the fictitious details we provided got us off the hook. I was nineteen. In preparation for the trial, the four of us from Mbekweni consulted a spiritual healer to help us win the trial. We did not advise the others to do so as they were all coloureds. When we met on the day of the trial, we all laughed after discovering that Kenny carried a small bottle in his pocket to help him win. Mr. Siraj Desai, currently a judge in the Supreme Court, was our lawyer. Desai skillfully outclassed the prosecutor by taking one of the pamphlets found in the garage and writing a song on the reverse – 'O What a Night'. He then requested the witness, Mr. Daniels, to read out loud what was written on the paper. He sounded very stupid when he read out the song. Desai did this to show that we were merely having a social gathering and were not discussing politics. The magistrate acquitted us.

Our arrest did not deter us from continuing with engagements. We were totally committed to the struggle and kept students busy with cultural activities during the school boycott.

Someone came up with the idea of showing films for a low admission fee. One of the students, David Mathokazi, knew someone who owned a projector. Along with David, Ndodomzi, Mthetheleli and Joe, I drove my father's car without a licence to collect the projector and was caught in a speed trap. A traffic officer flagged me down but I was too terrified to stop. He gave chase and I eventually managed to park the vehicle in one of the bays at Textile Factory in Jan van Riebeeck Street.

An elderly security guard refused to let us hide inside the factory so we all agreed to tell the traffic officers that we had no idea of the driver's name and that he was in the factory. I threw the keys under the car just before the officers arrived. They asked which one of us was the driver and demanded to look in the boot.

David panicked when the police threatened to lock us all up if we did not identify the driver. He wanted to get it over with as quickly as possible and tell them that he had driven the car. We tried persuading an African policeman to ask his white colleagues to let the matter drop but he ended up making things even worse, telling them that the car had been there since the previous day. Of course, they did not buy that. Ndodomzi indicated that David was the driver. I'm ashamed to say that I kept quiet, hoping that the police would give up. I was petrified of getting into trouble with the law again and possibly being arrested for my political activities. One of the officers gave David a ticket, fining him R150 for speeding and driving without a licence. Hoping against hope, I raised my hand when he eventually asked which one of us possessed a driver's licence. Fortunately, he did not ask me to produce it.

None of us had anywhere near enough money to pay David's fine so he arranged to see the prosecutor, who reduced the amount to R75. We could not raise that either. David eventually managed to secure the funds himself but came looking for us later, armed with four nails and threatening to hammer them into us for letting him down. Somehow, we managed to calm him down and convinced him that there was no way we could repay the money.

COSAS held a conference at Wilgespruit in May 1981, shortly before Republic Day. I was part of a delegation from the Western Cape who attended. David Jacobs, Andile Apleni and Andile Mrubata from Cape Town were there as observers as COSAS did not have a branch in the city at that time.

Under instructions from the National Executive Committee we travelled to Wits University in Johannesburg on Republic Day to *toyi–toyi* on the campus and protest by burning the old South African flag. *Toyi–toyi* was a form of dance practiced in the sixties by the liberation armies of Joshua Nkomo and Robert Mugabe during the struggle for independence in Rhodesia (now Zimbabwe). The dance was developed to boost soldiers' morale, instil a fighting spirit and increase their desire to overcome. Through association with Nkomo's forces and the sharing of military camps, the practice spilled over to uMkhonto weSizwe (MK) and spread like wildfire into the ranks of other political organizations, trade unions and student bodies around South Africa.

Republic Day was celebrated by white South Africans to commemorate the country's independence from British rule. For the blacks, this was a mockery. How could we celebrate our own oppression?

At Wits University we dealt with resistance from a few white students, one of whom was very brave. He tried snatching the flag from us but we gave him a beating before security guards took him away and called the police. Protesters scattered in different directions. Our group headed towards Johannesburg Station and spotted Jabu Ngwenya – one of the local protesters – inside a shop not far from the university. He stood casually combing his long hair, pretending not to have taken part in the disruptions. Jabu's ploy must have paid off because he was not apprehended.

We finally managed to reach the railway station and boarded the train to Cape Town. Afraid of being arrested, or worse, I panicked after hearing that the event had appeared on national television where I could clearly be seen burning the flag. The Special Security Branch had photos of the event and made every effort to hunt down the protesters. Rather than suffer constant harassment, many of our members left South Africa after the protest.

Back home, we remained underground as much as possible but were exposed during the day when we went to school. The Security Branch tried arresting and detaining me with no success and even turned up at my school one day but the gates had been locked.

At this point, it is important to mention Makhosi Ndzuzo and Bram Mhlom, two teachers who played a very instrumental role in giving us guidance while sharing in our cause. They warned us to be careful not to allow individual members to use student politics as a means of settling personal grudges, advised us to discourage students with destructive ideas from influencing others and urged us to make sure that we did not digress from our main purpose. No amount of words can express the invaluable contribution these teachers made.

I barely escaped arrest once again while driving Mr. Matshotyana's car. He was a friend of my father's and an ex–policeman, serving a term in prison for a criminal offense. I was bringing his wife back from town (still without a driving licence). Sometime earlier, she had asked my father if I could stay with her for a while and we were now on our way home after purchasing supplies for the small *spaza* (informal) shop they ran from their home. Mr. Mngqibisa of the Special Security Branch flagged me down and I seem to remember that he was with another policeman at the time. Mrs. Matshotyana persuaded them to let me drop her at home first, after which they were free to detain me. I drove straight to the school afterwards, pursuers hot on my heels. When we arrived I leapt out of the car and ran onto the school premises. Norman Ncaca, one of the teachers, quickly locked the gate when he saw the police chasing me. Because of the boycott, the teachers were standing around outside. Mrs. Matshotyana drove herself home. She did not have a licence either. Mngqibisa was furious but had no choice other than to leave without me.

At that time we had very dedicated members in Paarl East, particularly Allan Paulse who displayed outstanding leadership qualities. These members were responsible for mobilizing coloured schools and, although they encountered some resistance, finally managed to win a few over.

Certain coloured families disliked africans, calling us '*kaffirs*' (a derogatory term originally derived from the Arabic word *kafir* meaning ' unbeliever' or 'infidel'). They persuaded their children not to associate with us because we were seen as disruptive. I remember one incident that took place when we visited a friend at his home. His parents openly called us '*kaffirs*' and this caused him great embarrassment. It was the same with Patrick Ricketts's sister. She hated us passionately. Patrick had a great sense of humour and always managed to reduce her attempts at belittling us to nothing. She was probably being over–protective of her brother and certainly did not support our cause. Nevertheless we were determined to continue with the struggle, irrespective of whether people loved or hated us. None of us judged another from his or her family's perspective.

Allan Paulse's parents were a great comfort. They were very warm and understanding, to such an extent that we always felt we were part of the family. Joe Patel's family treated us extremely well too. We simply had to accept that some people are welcoming and supportive and others despised and discriminated against us on the basis of skin colour or opposing political beliefs. A few even threatened to call the police when they saw us.

CHAPTER 4

Studying in the Transkei

In 1982, Mthetheleli and I were sent to school at Gcinubuzwe Senior Secondary in Lady Frere, about 35 kilometres from Queenstown. I was in Grade 11 and Mthetheleli in Grade 12. Officers from the Special Branch arrived at the school one day wanting to see my passport, which I promptly produced. They told me that schools were not disrupted and burnt in their country and if they were ever made aware of any boycotts in the area, I would be detained immediately. Apparently, someone informed them that I was a political activist. Needless to say, I conducted my activities in the utmost secrecy after that, only approaching individuals whom I identified as having potential. History students were the easiest to approach.

On another occasion, the police arrived asking permission from the principal to speak to me. They went even further, driving me to my home so they could check my passport. Mthetheleli and I rented a house in Cumakala village, not far from the school. As we drove off a teacher named Mr. Shauza, who taught Biblical Studies, ran out and tried to stop us but the policemen ignored him. Glancing back I saw Mr. Shauza standing absolutely still, looking very worried. To my mind his expression meant only one of two things – prison or death.

Something strange happened as I was about to unlock the door to our house. One of Mthetheleli's classmates came running up with a key saying that she had to pick up a schoolbook for him. The police allowed

Sindiswa to go in first but she came back out again within a few minutes. I went to my room alone to fetch my travel documents and handed them over. Thankfully, everything was in order so the police left.

Wanting to allay my sneaking suspicions afterwards, I searched the entire room and was devastated to find *dagga* (marijuana) in Mthetheleli's suitcase. He was like my own brother so I confronted Sindiswa later on and she told me what had happened. Mthetheleli discovered that the police were going to take me back to the house and asked her to hide the dagga in a safe place. Furious, I demanded an explanation from my friend. He confessed and promised to get rid of the stuff and never smoke it again. To my knowledge, he honoured his promise. I came very close to being imprisoned for his crime that day.

As the year progressed life became increasingly difficult for the students. We could barely afford basic foodstuffs. Family members sent a little money whenever possible but it disappeared into the deep pockets of certain Post Office officials. Queries and confrontation proved a complete waste of time and effort. It was so frustrating. Mthetheleli and I gradually developed survival skills, befriending students whose families owned shops and assisting others with their studies – for a fee, or during the evenings when a meal was virtually guaranteed. Prior to this we often went without food for days, drinking diluted solutions of sugar and salt. Sipho Hlathi, a fellow student, suggested eating cheap glucose sweets and wrapping our bellies in tight bandages to ward off the hunger pangs. Psychologically, his method worked like a charm. We were occasionally lucky enough to be invited to someone's home when a ritual animal sacrifice took place – to share in the 'meal of the day'.

At times Reverend Mtini, a family relative from Lady Frere, would visit and kindly give me a little money. Our parents had great difficulty in providing us with clothing, especially our expensive school uniforms. Between us Mthetheleli and I owned five pairs of trousers – two grey and two khaki pairs for weekdays and one in navy blue that we shared on weekends. Coming from a poor background helped somewhat and there were more important issues to worry about than clothing.

I became increasingly aware of social and economic imbalances during my time in the Transkei and came into contact with the harsh realities of abject poverty, particularly at Cumakala Village. Rural conditions were far worse than in the towns and cities that I was used to. My number one priority was to pass Grade 11. I was aware that a good education would shape my political future, enable me to adequately tutor the students I had targeted and allow me to take part in my people's struggle for freedom. It was wonderful to discover that I had passed after receiving my results at home in Mbekweni during the December school holidays.

Soccer, swimming, rugby, karate, judo and weight lifting – I participated in them all. My father was a well–known sportsman who played for the black Springbok Rugby team in the '60s – honoured and acknowledged in 2001 when he received his Springbok blazer for lifetime achievement. His love of sport rubbed off onto me. As a youngster I played rugby with a plastic milk bottle stuffed with newspapers, or made full use of a tennis ball instead. My friends and I practiced on an open field minus our jerseys and T–shirts – in case they tore during one of our rather vigorous match disputes.

As far as swimming goes; I hated it at first. My father would throw me into the water, leaving me to struggle on my own in a desperate attempt to save myself from drowning. Paddling did not help. Water poured into my mouth and drowning seemed imminently possible. My father swam up and simply threw me a bit further – over and over again – shouting all the time. After learning to swim things looked decidedly brighter and I spent many wonderful hours having fun in the water with my friends. Ever since I narrated this story to my son Thando, and whenever we go to the beach, he always insists that I throw him in the water so he can learn to swim just like his dad.

One day, my friends and I played karate on a rustic boat made from two welded drums. My opponent kicked me and I fell into the water with one toe stuck firmly in between the drums. With my head underwater I had no choice but to pull the toe out as forcefully as possible, losing half of it in the process. Blood pouring from the wound, one courageous boy called Meshack Mcingana hoisted me onto his back and carried me home. After pouring paraffin over the wound, my family rushed me to Paarl General Hospital. Waiting for treatment, I heard another patient screaming at the top of his lungs. After discovering that he was in for stitches too, no one could hold me down. My family medicated the wound at home with a creative combination of patent and herbal remedies. Fortunately, the injury did not discourage me from swimming again.

Crime rates were far lower in those days. Children took part in many activities, ranging from drama and choral music to sport. I played soccer for Eleven Ideas (Sunlight) and rugby for Blues Rugby Football Club – later becoming a founder member of 'Izibane' (Highlights) the first non–racial team established in Mbekweni. Makhosi Ndzuzo, Bram Mhlom and Julius Allah formed this team. The experience helped me to excel in both rugby and soccer in the Transkei. I would play a rugby match and, immediately afterwards, join in the second half of a soccer match.

Mthetheleli and I were household names when it came to sport, particularly around the Lady Frere area. One day our school took part in a rugby match against Zwartwater. Because I was known as a skilled fly half, they secretly invited a soldier from the Transkei Defence Force to play in their team, instructing him to 'disorganize' me. He fractured my shoulder blade during a tackle. This happened shortly before the game ended, when the score was 30–0 in our favour. Changing position to play full back instead, I grabbed the ball with my sound hand and kicked but was unable to score another goal. A teacher took me to Glen Grey Hospital where the doctor warned me not to play any sport until the fracture had healed properly.

One day Clarkbury High pupils threw stones at us during an inter–school match after it became increasingly obvious that we would win the game. The match ended very abruptly.

During a game against Rubusana High School in Queensdale I kicked a decisive drop goal over the poles but the referee disqualified it. Before the principal intervened, pandemonium erupted when outraged fans ran onto the field. Although our team players were very committed we still lost the match. I have vivid memories of fans cheering us on, both inside and outside school premises. It was an incredible feeling, almost as if we were professional stars. I shall never forget it.

CHAPTER 5

Finally Leaving the Country

In December 1982 the University of Durban hosted a COSAS conference. News of the Lesotho massacre broke out during the conference. The South African Defence Force had murdered a group of ANC refugees in a raid in Lesotho. Our mood changed dramatically – anger and shock visible on everyone's faces. On returning home after the conference, we made up our minds to leave South Africa as soon as possible and worked extra hard to find contacts in neighbouring states. On Christmas day we slept at Vivian Matthee's home in Paarl East and prepared to go into exile. Patrick led and coordinated the operation.

We were reminded to observe strict secrecy and not talk about our plans to anyone who was not part of the group. On the morning of the

Farieda Ricketts

26th one of our comrades informed us that he had changed his mind, saying that he would rather pursue his education. His decision to stay behind disturbed us. Political exiles were regarded as terrorists. We feared that, if apprehended, he might spill the beans to the police. Regardless of the increased risk we went ahead with our plan. On the 26th Patrick and Farieda Ricketts, Vivian Matthee and Norman Petersen

27

boarded the train at Wellington Station. Patrick had married Farieda shortly before Christmas. Lloyd Fortuin drove Lucky Madubula and I to Worcester Station where we caught the same train en route to Botswana.

This is a poem that Farieda wrote about that long–awaited day:

We left in a group on the 26ᵗʰ December 1982 that summer evening, not knowing at the time that we would all be separated and face different kinds of music. We sat in separate seats on the train in the hope of not being detected. Our destination lay to the north. We were on our way to Botswana to join uMkhonto weSizwe and contribute to the struggle.

NORTH

Boarding the train is a relief
But finding a place to relax
Another matter
A seat at last!

The trip is strange
I do not know Jama
And he does not know me
Jama does not know Pat
Nor does he know Vivi.

Jama, Normie and Lucky are black
We are not that black
Separated on this train
We enter this new life
All with our own thoughts.

Jama and Normie are somewhere
Somewhere on this train
Sitting with them or speaking to them
Might be a crime
Or give our plan away.

The train must go on
We must reach the border
And step over
The AK–47 is waiting!

We need to prepare
To make our contribution
No matter how small.

We travelled in separate compartments and developed a secret sign for indicating the need to meet. Meetings were held between carriages. At Ramathlabama border post we registered as visiting tourists and entered Botwana without a hitch. Lucky and I held Transkeian passports. Patrick, Farieda, Norman and Vivian had South African ones. At that time it was difficult for political activists to obtain South African passports. The authorities issued them to some people but not to others and no one knew what criteria they used to discriminate between applicants. Arriving safely in Gaberone we hugged one another, shouting that we had finally made it after all these years.

A man we presumed to be an ANC official took us to an underground house where we met comrade Gideon. He gave us tips on what to do in the event of enemy attack, stressed the importance of discipline, told us about uMkhonto weSizwe; what the ANC training camps were all about and what was expected of us as civilians going into that environment. To our surprise we found out that he was a new recruit as well, preparing to go to Angola.

We were moved to the house of a coloured comrade known as Garnett 'Allan' Godden. Billy Masethla from the Security Department arrived to write our biographies before we underwent a crash course in the use of an AK–47. It was very exciting. The experience of touching a weapon for the first time was exhilarating. I felt that this gave us the power to achieve anything. Allan made our stay very comfortable, occasionally driving us to Maruapula High School for a swim.

After a week in Botswana everyone – except Lucky and I – was taken to Zambia for training. By the second week I was fed up and complained that we had not come all the way from South Africa to stay in Botswana – we wanted to be trained as well. If they did not take us to Angola, we would both head straight back to South Africa. Fortunately, they acceded to my request.

We boarded a ten–seater flight to Zambia. It was our very first experience of flying and we were amazed to see a black pilot. There were none in South Africa. In fact we had never even seen a photo of one in a magazine or book before. At that point it hit me – we were no longer in South Africa. This was my first real taste of freedom.

Zambian customs officials arrested and detained us until the following day. Zambia did not recognize Transkeian passports so we spent an uncomfortable night on a couch at the airport. The following day an ANC official arrived, sorted out the problem and took us to a restaurant for a well–earned meal.

We lived in an underground house for a short period of time. The commander responsible for our accommodation told us a lot of scary stories about the camp, so much so that we entertained second thoughts. There were two options – army training or completing our education, and he had to be completely sure of our total commitment. We made up our minds.

On the flight to Angola I ended up sitting next to a woman from Mozambique who only spoke Portuguese. We communicated with the help of a comrade named Crossby. She invited me to visit if I was ever in her part of the world and wrote her address on a slip of paper.

CHAPTER 6

Military Training in Angola

We were taken to the ANC transit camp at Viana which is a few kilometers outside Luanda, the capital of Angola, and two or three kilometers from a SWAPO (South West African People's Organization) refugee camp. Unofficially used for soldiers, Viana masqueraded as a civilian camp. During the day guards sat with their weapons concealed from view, sometimes playing soccer. One never suspected that they carried guns or that the camp housed an armoury. MK soldiers chosen to undergo further training were taken there first. All necessary documentation and air tickets were issued from there as well. New recruits from South Africa were sent on to Caculama Training Camp in the Eastern Province of Angola.

At Viana all new recruits underwent a body search, one by one. I suddenly remembered the address that the woman on the plane had given me and quickly threw the piece of paper away before my turn arrived. Declaring, or not declaring, her address was equally dangerous. They might have thought I was an enemy agent communicating with South Africa via Mozambique. No one was allowed to make contact with anyone outside the camp without the ANC's express permission. Mistakes cost people their lives. After the search, it occurred to me that I could have ended up in Quattro Prison if anyone had noticed me throwing the paper away.

Officers briefed us about the military and subjected us to rigorous physical training. I will never forget the time they staged an incredibly realistic mock attack. Fires burned, sirens wailed, tracer bullets flew all over the camp, bazookas fired and soldiers screamed. I swear that I smelled death that day. Experienced soldiers led us to a dugout where we took cover until all was clear. We laughed about it afterwards because a few of the recruits were half–naked at the time of the 'attack' and others were bleeding from wounds inflicted when they frantically ran for cover.

Physical training took place in the early mornings. If we showed signs of fatigue the instructors commanded us to pick up the pace, shouting *"Uyaloya!"* meaning "You are a witch!" This insult referred to people who were down–spirited, fragile or lacked commitment. At one stage a man in my group stumbled and fell. One of the instructors told him to get up and run. While he was still on the ground the instructor fired a shot. Our fallen comrade jumped up and ran. Despite the hardship and deprivation, they certainly prepared us for the additional rigours of future training camps.

Ad–hoc tasks kept us occupied during the day. We wrote our biographies for the third time. There was always a risk of informers infiltrating the camps so all facts contained in the three biographies were checked for consistency.

Viana taught me to appreciate uMkhonto weSizwe. It was here that I first saw MK soldiers in uniform. Carrying an AK–47 gave me a sense of pride and determination and I never doubted the MK's ability to overthrow the apartheid regime.

Viana accommodated trained soldiers as well as recruits like myself. Occasionally, delegations such as the International Red Cross arrived from Geneva to inspect the camp and the items they had supplied to the 'refugees' – trucks, food and clothing. International communities sympathetic to our plight donated the goods. Prior to each visit we cleaned up and made sure that nothing of a military nature was visible, including soldiers in uniform. For a short while, Viana resembled nothing more than a refugee camp.

During the months we spent there – from January to March 1983 – everyone's morale was very high. We held evening 'sing–songs' in a dry swimming pool and sometimes played soccer with SWAPO soldiers, who always defeated us because they had a lot more stamina. During the day we were kept busy cleaning the camp. At lunchtimes we queued up in the open air for a meal of porridge or rice with tinned meat, followed by baked bread, tea and coffee. Afterwards we relaxed on stretchers and read books. Fresh meat was available whenever we celebrated events of national or international importance. Pigs were sometimes slaughtered and we enjoyed a real feast.

The weather was always extremely hot, bringing hordes of unwanted buzzing visitors. A mobile tank provided fresh water for the camp, towed in by tractor. We washed with cold water in the mornings in an open space partly concealed by a 1,5 metre high wall. Toilet facilities consisted of two parallel planks suspended over a big hole dug for the purpose, approximately 500 metres from the camp but only a few metres away from a tree where a security guard always stood on duty.

It was at Viana that I first saw Oliver Tambo, respected african leader and intellectual – the president of the ANC. He was a well–built man who wore glasses – humble, persuasive and a decisive visionary. Whenever he paid a visit to another country he always brought something back – in the form of pledges or commitments that enabled us to train soldiers or buy materials. When it came to military discipline he was extremely outspoken, reminding us that our fight was not against whites but a regime. He believed that the white community was totally ignorant of the fact that they too lived under oppression and were afraid to voice their feelings, supporting an illegitimate regime and accepting its propaganda.

Tambo came to the camp heavily guarded by armed MK soldiers called 'The Young Pioneers', who made an incredible impression on me. Completely focused young men, they were clearly determined to provide the utmost security for our president. Oliver Tambo addressed us in the hall, speaking about the state of our struggle and the obstacles we faced at the time. In great pain he added that Samora Machel, president of Mozambique, had recently signed the 'Komati Accord' with South Africa in an attempt to remove the ANC from Mozambique. Tambo was deeply hurt by Machel's failure to communicate with the ANC in good faith. I remember him pointing to the ground and saying that the Botha regime had made a coffin for the ANC but we would never be buried in it. The more he spoke, the more excited I grew. He stressed the word 'precision' three times, impressing us with the need to be precise in our struggle and our determination to destroy apartheid.

Jonas Gwangwa (one of my favourite artists) and the ANC cultural group once performed on stage at Viana Camp. The group toured different countries, campaigning for material support for the ANC. In their capacity as entertainers they were treated like civilians, although most of them were trained soldiers. Highlighting our plight through music and drama, they showed the world the cultural heritage of our people in South Africa. Gwangwa knew his trombone like the palm of his hand and also sang with deep emotion, reflecting the suffering of so many South Africans. His music and singing touched us all. Far from home and those we loved, life in exile was never easy. I salute all the men and women who did our country proud and showed astounding commitment under such abnormal conditions.

Patrick was moved to Caculama Training Camp. Farieda left for Caxito, leaving me behind at Viana Transit Camp. Lucky, Vivian and Norman were taken to Caculama as well. Patrick rejoined me at Viana later and then we were both transferred to Caxito. Our formal military training took place there.

Caxito was outside Luanda, close to Viana. An armed escort transported us to the camp in a Gaz truck. The drive through thick bush was a bit tense, being the perfect cover for a UNITA (National Union for Total Independence of Angola) ambush. We were not armed but I would have been far more comfortable carrying my AK–47. Our enemies were unpredictable. We seldom knew where, or when, they would launch an attack.

There was always great excitement whenever our leaders paid a visit to the camp. They boosted morale and kept us up to date on the state of affairs in South Africa and neighbouring countries. The oppressed people of our country were pleading for us to intensify the struggle. Our leaders kept on emphasizing the need for discipline; we were to obey instructions, apply underground rules to the full and not betray the ANC under any circumstance. Some of our units failed to do so and, as a result, were withdrawn from South African operations. Leaders expressed concern about the high rate of comrades who were either arrested, killed or turned *askari* around the Swaziland and Botswana borders. *Askaris* were MK soldiers who turned against the ANC and joined forces with the apartheid police, helping them to capture other comrades. For whatever reasons, soldiers within our own ranks were working for the apartheid regime. Some did so willingly. Others were forced under torture. A few of our men died under mysterious circumstances. We were warned to exercise extreme caution, particularly with regards to women who might work for the security police, using seduction to lure us into a trap.

Andile Ndzanga, known in MK circles as Toks, was the camp commander, later replaced by Ben Litch. Armed guards protected the area around the clock. The armoury stood between the kitchen and administration buildings, very close to a guardhouse and the commander's bunker that was camouflaged with soil–covered logs. First used as an underground camp, soldiers were trained at Caxito before being returned to South Africa. By limiting exposure, risks were minimized so the various units were kept apart from one another. If any soldiers were captured they would not be able to give out information regarding the others. Great fighters such as Solomon Kalushi Mahlangu and Barney Moloikwane were trained here. One of the MK's most respected military commanders, Barney led a special unit that carried out a wide range of attacks in South Africa.

Later on Patrick and Farieda left the camp. I was promoted to Platoon Commander with Mzukisi Skweyiya from Mdantsane as my deputy. His MK name was Thandisizwe Zembe. We found ourselves in the company of devoted men like Patrick Mangashe and Xolile Matebese, both of whom excelled at their jobs. A highly disciplined medical officer, Mangashe treated his patients with utmost care and dignity. He fed them personally and kept the hospital tent spotlessly clean. Matebese was our kitchen commander. Meals were served at specific times and I often felt very hungry in between. He helped me out many a time and never hesitated to fill the empty gap in my stomach.

Jackie Selebe (currently National Commissioner for the South African Police Services), Xolile Majeke and Manala Manzini joined us, sharing their experiences and political maturity. I learned a great deal from them. Even though all three men were far more politically advanced than myself, they were under my command. They told us what had happened in South Africa during the nineteen sixties and earlier. At some stage Jackie contracted malaria. To the best of my knowledge he was the only soldier at Caxito to be issued with an extra–large uniform (donated by the German Democratic Republic). Within a short time the disease ravaged his huge body.

Female comrades joined the camp as well, including Nomfundo Fazzie (Nokhaya Nxele) from the Eastern Cape, Nonkonzo Matobako (Ruth Mazibuko), Nompumelelo Matobako (Sizakele Ngcobo) and Khosi Nyoka (Thuli), all from KwaZulu Natal. Thuli was part of a unit of MK soldiers who were betrayed by informers. Security forces ambushed them inside South Africa. Brave and serious, she was very bitter about the apartheid regime and wanted nothing more than to play a part in liberating her oppressed people.

Sometime later an Afrikaans–speaking female named Flou arrived, but could not last the pace. She eventually left the camp for better medical treatment after contracting malaria. She used to scream hysterically and was completely uncontrollable. African women fell ill too, but stoically bore the pain and learnt to live with it, determined to complete their training. They were women of substance who expected no pity and took part in exactly the same activities as male soldiers. I applaud them for their amazing courage and determination.

Inevitably, women soldiers were subjected to amorous proposals from time to time but generally behaved themselves in a manner befitting the army. Rejected suitors occasionally spread malicious rumours about females who refused their advances but the women were undeterred by the gossip. Demand exceeded supply. There were far fewer female than male soldiers so they were regarded as valuable assets. Those who did have love affairs conducted them discreetly, respecting the feelings of those outside a relationship. Not a single altercation took place in which a woman was the cause.

Slogans were very popular at Caxito, although the camp administration banned a few of them. Whenever a bell rang we shouted, *"Ngenye imini iyokhala ndingekho!"* ("One day it will ring in my absence"). Another banned slogan was *"Mangibuka lezi ntaba kusengathi ziyasondela"* ("When I look at these hills, they seem to come closer"). Officials automatically assumed that the slogans had negative connotations but that was not the case. The administration building stood on a series of hills. All decisions, selections and recommendations as to which units would be leaving to fight in South Africa took place here. They were our *HILLS OF HOPE.*

We had another saying as well; in the ANC one plus one did not always add up to two – because nothing could be regarded as a certainty. One might receive orders to deploy the following day but end up staying in camp for a year or more.

As Platoon Commander one of my duties involved deploying unit members to various guard posts and drawing up timetables listing names, times and durations of the various posts. On one particular day an instruction arrived from Staff Commander Sithembiso (the officer on duty that day) to send Nonkonzo Matobako (Ruth Mazibuko) to a certain post at midnight, probably with an ulterior motive. Deployment was my responsibility, not his, so I asked for clarification. He insisted that I carry out the instruction. Quite sure that Sithembiso was abusing his authority, and having my platoon's welfare at heart, I refused. That evening the entire camp was summoned to a procedural roll call. Sithembiso told me to remain behind after all the other platoons were dismissed. He demanded to know why I had defied his order. Without giving me a chance to answer he slapped my face – hard. Utterly humiliated, I nevertheless managed a degree of composure before replying, "I joined uMkhonto weSizwe on the understanding that it was a political organization and a disciplined army. I am not a common criminal!" Turning away, I left him standing motionless and wide–eyed and returned to base, asking my deputy to take over my responsibilities for that evening.

Unknown to me, Mshoshovu, the Deputy Officer on duty, saw the entire incident and reported it to his superior. Ben Litch and Camp Commissar Herman called Sithembiso and I to the administration block, wanting to find out exactly what had happened. We both had the opportunity of presenting our case. Sithembiso told the truth, confessing that he had been in the wrong. Even so, attending the session appeared to be a total waste of time as no one showed any sign of taking the matter seriously. I left feeling worse than before.

The following morning the entire camp was ordered to meet at our general gathering point. Litch informed everyone of the previous evening's incident, highlighting the fact that the Staff Commander was an old soldier who was supposed to set an example and, in addition, assaulting an MK officer was a serious and unacceptable offense – an abuse of power that would not be tolerated in the people's army. He reminded us that uMkhonto weSizwe had been formed to defend the people of South Africa against oppression, not for personal gain. Sithembiso was summarily disarmed, demoted and ordered to join my platoon, reporting directly to me. The camp administrators rectified his 'misunderstanding' of military discipline, sending him to the new recruits unit to suffer the indignity of repeating three months basic training.

Afterwards Litch complimented me for displaying maturity and calmness and said that he expected me to guide my comrade and teach him how to be a proper soldier. He called Sithembiso to attention and instructed him to report to his new Platoon Commander. Bravely, he marched over and faced me, at attention, saying, "Comrade Commander, with your permission – may I join your platoon?" I replied, "At ease comrade, you may join." Ben Litch earned my respect that day for the manner in which he handled the situation and I admired Sithembiso for his humility. The step had been necessary and served to get the message across to other army members as well. I sat down with my comrade later, assuring him that I held no grudges and he would not be victimized. I lived up to that promise.

Sometime later Sithembiso became a tactics instructor. One day he left a defensive F1 grenade booby–trapped in the bush, intending to kill a large animal for meat. That evening the entire class had to find and disarm the grenade and bring it back to camp. If only one or two men had gone, UNITA soldiers could easily have captured or kidnapped them. Travelling in a group meant better safety and security. Sithembiso was punished for his dangerous mistake. Had an unsuspecting MK soldier walked along that route, he may have been blown to pieces in the ensuing explosion.

Another soldier named Weaver gave me problems as well. He worked in the kitchen and tended to make a nuisance of himself in the women's quarters, normally staying until late at night. The women voiced their disapproval but he refused to listen. They brought this to my attention so I immediately intervened, warning him to respect their privacy and leave when asked to do so. He was furious and very insolent. Although Weaver was not a member of my platoon, I was expected to address any complaint that came my way. Ben Litch tied him to a tree for a few hours to cool down but I did not approve of this type of punishment and felt personally responsible.

At Caxito, we received comprehensive training in military engineering, firearms, politics, tactics, military combat work (MCW) and topography. After completing my training I went on to specialize in Military Engineering where we dealt with the following topics:

- Safety rules for handling explosives
- Types of explosives and detonators
- Formulae for the destruction of property
- Manual and remote detonation
- Propellant charges
- Homemade explosives

We were taught to handle light and heavy firearms and learned about safety procedures, magazine loading and re–loading, assembling and disassembling and shooting positions. During political classes, we studied the history of the ANC, the South African Communist Party and trade unionism. We learnt about the Freedom Charter, resistance wars in SA, ANC strategy and tactics and were introduced to Marx and Lenin. We learnt how to use a compass and binoculars, how to read maps and study terrain and elevations. We were taught about armed engagement – penetration, retreat, reconnaissance, camouflage, formation and marching drills.

Mock attacks took place as well. Whenever the alarm bell sounded everyone took cover instantly. After the all–clear we reported at the central gathering point. During one of these exercises Thandisizwe, who was also a former boxing champion, dived straight into a pool of mud and caused great hilarity when he arrived covered in the stuff and looking very embarrassed.

Patrick, Farieda and I did our basic training together. Farieda had contracted malaria and her health deteriorated. Shortly before a practical tactics session, she suffered another bout of fever but our instructor insisted that she take part in the exercise, regardless of the fact that we were using live ammunition and had no protection for our ears. This particular exercise was known as 'Penetration' – surprise attacks on the enemy followed by immediate retreat. One soldier carried a PKM machine gun, some of us had AK–47s and Farieda was issued with an RPG–7 rocket launcher. We all had to keep our mouths wide open in order to prevent damage to our eardrums. Farieda was to start the firing. Some of us were to coordinate our firing, attack and then retreat. The soldier with the machine gun, along with other men armed with AK –47s, would provide us with cover.

Holding the loaded RPG–7, Farieda stood there – motionless. Suddenly the weapon flew into the air. Everyone dived for cover. Fortunately it landed on the ground without exploding. The exercise was completed without her.

On the way back to camp, Farieda battled to keep up. Our instructor ordered me to tie a rope around her waist and pull her along because she was delaying the whole group. This put me in a very difficult position. I knew she had a fever and her husband was my friend, but I had to obey a direct order. Patrick was very understanding and mature and never once took the incident personally. Exile made you – or broke you. Survival depended on the strength of one's political convictions, one's commitment to the cause and one's understanding of political and social dynamics.

The most frightening aspect of our training involved defusing explosive devices. If a device had not exploded after fifteen minutes it was deemed safe to approach – with extreme caution. We always exercised maximum concentration, being very careful not to take any chances. One only had to make a single mistake and it could cost one's life. There were no second chances.

Patrick and I often shared all–night guard duties, brewing tea over a small fire and chatting to one another to keep awake. Insects and other noisy night creatures kept watch as well. If the noise suddenly ceased, we knew someone was coming. Fortunately for us it was always the platoon commander or commissar, checking to find out if we were still awake.

There were exciting moments at the camp as well, particularly on days of national and international importance. Welcome Msomi (MK name), a talented musician from Soweto, came to entertain us with his trumpet. On the 16th of June we remembered Hector Peterson's untimely death during the Soweto uprisings, when he and many other students were massacred in a protest against the introduction of Afrikaans as the language of instruction in our schools. On the 1st of May we celebrated International Worker's Day and recognized contributions made by the working class in the liberation of exploited workers.

Drama was another important part of extra–curricular activities at Caxito, creating a much–appreciated diversion from everyday duties. On one of these occasions Patrick, Farieda and I took part in a play depicting the plight of black people in South Africa – dramatizing the effects of racialism and oppression. None of us had any acting experience but this made it even more poignant. Patrick played a typical white racist with Farieda in the role of a disadvantaged black mother struggling to earn a decent living and educate her son. I played her child. In one scene Patrick had to bump into Farieda, shouting insults. We knew only too well what that felt like.

During the week our soccer field doubled as a shooting range. Buck would sometimes saunter past the stationary target within the hundred–metre range, unwittingly providing a welcome change to our military diet.

As in most army camps, gossip and storytelling were rife. Newspapers were scarce and regarded as treasures. We craved news. Comrades pretending to know critical facts would get the attention they sought by spreading disinformation. Nevertheless we savoured and mulled over every report, whether true or not. 'Special Operations' were artillery specialists who conducted their activities from a secret base unknown to the rest of us. We all admired their courage. They boasted about travelling to South Africa from Angola, carrying out an operation and returning to camp on the same day. Whenever they arrived to collect ammunition from the armoury for target practice we hung on their every word.

Ordinary soldiers received no money for their services. The MK provided uniforms, food and toiletries. President Tambo approached international organizations such as the International Red Cross and

Anti–Apartheid Movement for assistance. Hoards of food and clothing arrived from different countries in support of our cause but not everything was suitable for use in the army. Men on survival courses outside the camp bartered with local peasants, exchanging unwanted items for the goods that we lacked.

Soldiers were permitted to fish in the river close to our kitchen. One day Sindy Mbobo (now a Colonel in the South African National Defence Force) and I went down to the river, choosing a nice secluded spot. The water looked so inviting that I stripped naked and dived in. It was just like being a child again – until Sindy screamed "Crocodile!" Panicking, I swam in the wrong direction. He yelled out, warning me that I was heading towards the UNITA side. I made a quick turnabout thinking that the 'crocodile' was between the opposite bank and me. Swimming downriver, I managed to find a shallow spot with low banks and scrambled out of the water as fast as possible.

Inevitably, I went down with malaria as well and was sent to Viana. Sindy (who was in Viana at the time) devoted his time and energy to caring for me. I could keep nothing down. He tried everything, including special foods purchased from the diplomatic shop. Some of my comrades had died from this dreadful disease and I firmly believed I was next in line. Sindy's care and devotion definitely saved my life.

On one occasion a unit of MK soldiers from Nampula in Mozambique appeared and had a heated argument with President Tambo, complaining about poor living conditions and claiming that promises had been made but not kept. The National Commissar, whose duties included looking after the political education and social welfare of our soldiers, had abandoned them in Mozambique. They were fed up and would rather go back to South Africa than starve to death in Nampula, struggling to feed and clothe themselves. Oliver Tambo gave the order for these men to receive further training at Caxito in preparation for fighting in South Africa. I was in command of their unit and sympathized with their frustrations. Ben Litch reminded me about the responsibility of command. These soldiers were angry so the inevitable problems of ill discipline needed to be addressed.

In December 1983 new recruits were being sent to Malange, the training camp at Caculama. UNITA was an illegitimate opposition army that rebelled against the MPLA (Popular Movement for the Liberation of Angola) government of Angola and terrorized the population. By that time they had already engaged uMkhonto weSizwe, killing many of our soldiers.

Still suffering the after–effects of malarial fever, I volunteered to help in recovering the bodies of our fallen comrades. Our convoy drove up to the battlefield in the Eastern Province of Angola. On the way to Caculama we had to drop off a group of new recruits from South Africa and joined up with trained comrades from the German Democratic Republic. One of our V8 Landrovers overturned. Fortunately, there was no major damage or loss of life. Afterwards we drove on to Cacuso in the same province but none of us could rest after discovering that our comrades had been killed in an ambush by UNITA troops. Arriving at Musafo Camp near Cacuso, 'Qothole' Gasa ecstatically welcomed us at the entrance, firing his rifle into the air in sheer excitement. No one raised an eyebrow, although such behaviour was strictly forbidden. Late that evening we joined forces with FAPLA (Popular Armed Forces for the Liberation of Angola) troops and proceeded into the bush in two large trucks, to the point where we believed the ambush had taken place.

No one had time to plan for this operation. We acted purely in anger and had no idea of the area's terrain, retreat routes or any other contingency in case of attack. There were no visible signs of available cover and it was pitch dark as well. Our engine noise carried over a large distance. FAPLA soldiers spoke nothing but Portuguese. Barely five kilometers away, a UNITA base stood on top of a hill. To say the least, our situation was somewhat tense. We had no idea how our fallen comrades came to be there in the first place. In a nutshell, we were virtually repeating their mistake. Beki, one of the men who survived the ambush and suffered a bullet wound in the foot, helped us to find the right spot. We came across two bodies in a terrible state of decay and decided to postpone further searching until daylight. Unknown to us, we left two wounded men behind in the dark. They heard us but were afraid to call out in case we were enemy soldiers.

An evacuated village provided shelter for the night. The following morning we combed the area, being very careful not to step on any mines. Although a reasonable force in terms of numbers, none of us wanted to be surprised by another ambush. We had no way of knowing whether UNITA troops were watching us or not. The heat was dreadful and crawling maggots infested the corpses. Using military canvas bags for stretchers, we carried five more bodies back to the open trucks. Luckily we also found the two wounded men that day. Jeff (an MK soldier) and a FAPLA soldier were the only survivors. When we arrived, both Jeff and the FAPLA soldier were sitting under a tree. Jeff was a medical officer and had his medical equipment with him. His head was bandaged and he held an FI defensive grenade in his hand. I assumed that he had bandaged himself.

Returning to the evacuated village we did everything possible to keep Jeff alive. Wounded in the head and stomach, all he wanted was a cigarette and a drink of water. He died later. We were terribly distressed to learn that our amateur ministrations, ignorance of human anatomy and lack of medical training hastened his death. We drove back to Cacuso and buried our comrades. I silently prayed that, if I died, it would be in South Africa and not in Angola – buried far from my family.

The return journey took us through a village populated mainly by women and children. UNITA forces had killed or imprisoned most of their menfolk. It was a poignant moment. The women jumped up and wept, hands on heads, cries ringing out their grief. They uttered words that many of us could not understand but we shared in their sorrow. It was a clear, stiflingly hot day. I stood in silence, bone–tired, sweating and deep in thought. This was the inescapable reality of death – the end–product of war. It was difficult to accept or come to terms with and brought home the deadly seriousness of my chosen career.

Angola was engaged in a vicious war. Many South Africans played a large part in the defence of her people, sacrificing ideals, life and youth without seeking praise or self–glory. Some comrades became drug addicts, criminals or hobos – but still deserve respect for their selfless efforts. South Africans can never erase the fact that the freedom they enjoy today is a direct result of yesterday's sacrifice.

An element of growing discontent among MK soldiers erupted in Angola towards the end of 1983. The men began to resent fighting in Angola when their own people needed them so desperately in South

Africa. We all went into exile to be trained and armed to fight at home. No one wanted to die in a foreign country.

ANC leaders briefed us when the trouble started and the National Executive gave orders to deal with the situation, warning that mutiny was punishable by death. Many of our troops were highly infiltrated and considered a military coup. Our leaders requested assistance from the MPLA government in disarming mutinous troops at Viana. The soldiers fought back, resulting in an exchange of gunfire before they were successfully disarmed. Some of them died in the process. Chris Hani tried to persuade the militants to submit to ANC command but his entreaty fell on deaf ears.

Soldiers carried out these acts under instruction. Whether they did so blindly or not is a different matter. The reality remains that many of them were victims of divisive propagandists using mob psychology to discredit the ANC and create an air of hopelessness. It was a sad day for uMkhonto weSizwe and the African National Congress.

Joe Modise was sent to ascertain which soldiers remained loyal to the ANC. He divided the soldiers into separate groups and sent them to different camps. Those sent to Pango overpowered the camp command and shot a few loyal ANC comrades while attempting to take over the administration. Staunch ANC members deployed from other camps dealt with the Pango rebels – some of whom were executed by firing squad. The situation was tense. Soldiers were not permitted to express any negativity but secretly continued to pray for the lives of their rebellious comrades. A cause that began as a genuine cry to defend the oppressed peoples of our country deteriorated into a massacre within its own ranks. I personally believe that we acted very harshly, yet it is easy to pass judgment in retrospect when one was not a witness to the event. Those who were confronted with the reality may well have been more justified in killing than in capturing.

There are so many other tales that could be told about our life in exile but we were not allowed to record our activities for security reasons and, unfortunately, some stories were inevitably lost.

CHAPTER 7

Preparing to Return to South Africa

Around March of 1984 Chris Hani, Joe Modise and Andrew Masondo came to Caxito after the mutiny was over, to interview soldiers wanting to return and fight in South Africa – myself included. We were summoned to face a panel and supply a motivation. I said that my resolve remained unchanged, regardless of the fact that I had initially expected a short period of training but had actually been in exile for more than a year.

The following weekend Madoda 'Isaac' Mnyamana told me that *Um–china* had arrived and my name was on the list! Back in South Africa – particularly in the Durban area – people played an illegal game similar to lotto. The 'china man' was the person responsible for paying out the winnings. In this particular instance it meant that I was one of the lucky people chosen to leave for South Africa.

That evening Andile Apleni took me from Viana. We drove to a place called 'The Plot'. When we arrived Mthetheleli Titana was there – half–asleep, waiting to be taken to the training camp. It was an unexpected reunion and he filled me in on the latest news. Large numbers of our comrades back in Paarl were leaving South Africa to join uMkhonto weSizwe – including my former girlfriend, Pamela Dlali. At that very moment she was on her way to join me in exile. Our paths were obviously doomed not to cross. Mthetheleli and I eventually said our goodbyes. He wished me well and we both agreed it would be preferable to return home together. Neither one of us knew what the future held. We could be shaking hands for the very last time.

It was unsafe to fly directly to South Africa from Angola as we were now officially classed as terrorists. Infiltrations took place overland from bordering countries such as Mozambique or Botswana or from either of the two countries within our country's borders – Lesotho and Swaziland. Our route would take us through Zambia and Botswana to the South African border at Ramathlabama.

My flight landed safely in Zambia. I was astounded to see Pamela at the airport, on her way to board a flight to Angola. To this day I do not know whether I did the right thing. I passed her without a word, not sure how to react. The meeting might simply have been a coincidence or it may have been a plan to test my underground discipline. Observing rules was a constant necessity. In public, every MK soldier had to pretend he did not know anyone around him, but the incident really bothered me. Sadly, I found out later that she took my silence personally, believing that I was no longer interested.

We faced different challenges in Zambia. Comrade Chips (MK name) narrowly escaped being killed by a soldier from the RC (Revolutionary Command). He offered to drive the man to a remote farm to deliver five litres of fish oil to his family. Along the way, his passenger asked to stop so he could relieve himself. Chips waited inside the car. The fellow came to the window claiming that one of the tyres was flat but when Chips went to investigate there was nothing wrong with it. Immediately suspicious, he searched the vehicle and found an AK–47 hidden under the soldier's jacket on the back seat. Ordering him into the boot, Chips drove back to the RC and handed him over to the ANC security officers.

In another incident in Zambia, soldier's allowances disappeared from the RC Commander's office. Our clothing and luggage were searched but nothing was found. Some time prior to this, one of the men mentioned that a big party had taken place at Kabwata, organized by the Commander. This seemed a bit suspicious but I thought it safer to keep quiet.

It was not the only episode involving Commander Sash. Joe Modise brought a beautiful yellow Safari land cruiser and parked it safely in the yard behind a corrugated iron gate every evening, under the watchful eye of a security guard. One day it simply disappeared. Shortly before that happened, Sash reported the vehicle's keys as missing. A few evenings later I spotted him in the distance driving very slowly past the security building. The following day Joe Modise and the Commander questioned our group, asking whether we knew anything about the missing vehicle. By this stage I was thoroughly sick and tired of all the implied accusations – first the missing allowances and now the land cruiser – and firmly told Modise that I was very surprised at his question. After all, Commander Sash had driven it away the previous evening. The perpetrator's face registered shock. He obviously thought no one had noticed him and probably hoped the guard on duty would be blamed instead. The stolen key story was merely a ruse to cover up his crime. Joe Modise asked me to supply him with the details. Sash started to walk away but Joe apprehended him and handed him over to the 'Imbokotho' – the security branch of the ANC. The Commander had sold the vehicle to a Zambian citizen but it was speedily recovered. This was an important lesson for me. I wondered how many other soldiers had been accused of crimes they did not commit.

Fortunately, not everything I experienced in Zambia was negative. One day we held a meeting at the ANC headquarters in Lusaka to discuss our problems. Oliver Tambo requested to say a few words. He spoke passionately about the role of sport and stressed its importance as a means of teaching discipline to the troops. Soldiers of the people's army should conduct themselves as representatives of South African people but, in general, our performance as sportsmen was poor. Comrades in Tanzania were doing very well and took part in local tournaments. He also mentioned that he used to play sport in his earlier days but, due to ill health, was forced to stop. He promised to address problems concerning the lack of transport, uniforms and a coach. These would be attended to when he went to Sweden. Tambo was a talented motivator who inspired and encouraged us and showed a great keenness to help – even with regards to sport. Tambo instructed Andrew Masondo to coach our team (called 'Moses Kotane') the following week. This made a tremendous difference to our game. Strangely enough whenever Tambo watched we played well – but as soon as he left we were defeated.

Vivian and I were sent to Mtendere where we met up with Mzukisi Sikweyiya (Thandisizwe Zembe) and his wife. Mzukisi had been my deputy at Caxito. One day he, his wife, a friend and I went to see a movie. As we stood in the queue two Zambians pushed Mzukisi's wife and a fight started. Other people in the queue cheered us on until the police were alerted. They produced official identification and ordered us to stop fighting. The four of us ran as fast as we could to the ANC headquarters. The same people who had been on our side earlier joined the chase. When the police arrived we decided not to create unnecessary problems for the ANC and submitted to arrest. At the police station we handed over our belts and shoes and they locked us up. The communal cell was dark. The floor was wet and it smelled terrible. The other prisoners became abusive but we could barely see them through the gloom. Mzukisi warned us to stick together. If we had to fight, we would do so. Fortunately, Thozamile Botha, a SACTU (South African Congress of Trade Unions) official, came to our rescue and the police released us.

During our stay at Mtendere we came into contact with very experienced MK soldiers and learnt a great deal from them. We lived like civilians with plenty of time to relax between March and June of 1984, occasionally listening to loud music emanating from a nearby *shebeen* (an informal township tavern or bar). This was the first time I heard 'Weekend Special' and 'Celebration' and I automatically presumed the singer was American. What a delight to learn later that it was our very own Brenda Fassie from South Africa, whom I knew in Cape Town as a stage actress. In exile, anything to do with home meant a great deal.

We drew up a duty roster so that everyone would know exactly when his turn to cook came around. The ANC provided weekly food supplies and an allowance for purchasing cigarettes and toiletries. Now and again local friends popped in for a visit, normally at meal-times. Our cooking was legendary. At night we took turns guarding the house. Security was a major concern and the same precautions were taken at every house that accommodated MK soldiers.

Returning home became an ever–increasing reality. We were almost there!

When we reached Botswana, we stayed at Broadhurst in the home of a staunch BNF (Botswana National Front) official. Patrick came to visit and gave me a good deal of encouragement. Later, we were moved to Mogoditsane. The family whom we stayed with treated us extremely well. A woman by the name of Thandi lived nearby and kindly offered to help me with whatever I needed. I really felt at home and was sad to leave this place, not knowing if I would ever meet my newfound friends again. My exile had lasted for one year and eight months.

CHAPTER 8

Infiltrating our Motherland

Vivian and I arrived back in South Africa in the middle of August 1984. We were escorted to the South Africa border and given enough money to pay for the rest of the journey. Apparently we were the first unit to enter the country via Botswana, on our way to Cape Town. Prior to this, units infiltrated from Lesotho. Gen. Lambrecht Moloi Lehlohonolo and Comrade Dan gave us our final briefing and then embraced us before saying goodbye.

I experienced mixed feelings that evening. Emotions vacillated between bravery and panic. I imagined myself liberating my people and saw their jubilation as they hailed all the freedom fighters as heroes. On the other hand, casualties around infiltration sites were high and I was afraid of being captured or killed. Here we were, given no choice as to our point of entry. Thoughts of friends and family went round and round in my head but I managed to compose myself. I was a soldier of the people's army – prepared to die for a noble cause.

It was very dark. The lights of Bophuthatswana glowed in the distance so we presumed this was the Ramathlabama border. We waited on the gravel road for our contact to arrive. A car approached after a few minutes. The driver switched on his hazard lights and said he would be driving us to the railway station at Kimberley. The poor man had flu and was obviously quite ill. I thought about offering to drive but decided against it, in case he suspected an ulterior motive.

We arrived at the station early the next morning and bought tickets to Cape Town. UMkhonto weSizwe taught us to be constantly aware of our surroundings. A Cressida was parked close to the pedestrian entrance. A white gentleman sat inside it reading a book. We had to pass the car on the way to the platform but he gave no indication of seeing us. Vivian and I climbed aboard the train, occupying seats far removed from one another.

After passing through Beaufort West, he told me that someone had spotted him so he would disembark at the next station, leaving me to hold onto his portion of the money. Although Vivian was my Commander, I insisted on staying together and putting up a fight if need be. Thankfully, he listened to my reasoning and eventually agreed. His confidence in me meant a lot and I will always be grateful for it.

When we reached Paarl, Garth Adams contacted Lloyd to arrange accommodation for Vivian in Paarl East. I contacted Radi Ndevu, whom I trusted implicitly, and gave him our brief. We had to establish an MK Command structure in the Western Cape and recruit and train new members. After secretly meeting with my father that night I went on to my cousin's husband, Dambile Kweleta, and spent the night at his home.

Around ten the next morning the police knocked on the door, wanting to search the place. Among them was an African detective named Mfamana. Managing to avoid detection, I ran into a room where my cousin's sister was busy washing herself and hid behind the door armed with two defensive grenades. The police checked all the other rooms as well as the backyard while Mhimhi spoke to Detective Mfamana, convincing him that she was alone in the house. Fortunately he believed her. If they had entered the room I was quite prepared to pull the pin.

We could never be sure whether our movements were observed or a comrade would betray us to save his own skin. We were now MK operatives who had illegally infiltrated our country. Very few comrades knew we had returned. When Max Kweleta gave me a lift into town I warned him not to tell a soul. During a spell in detention sometime later I found out that someone had spotted me in Cape Town and informed the Paarl Security Branch. The same thing happened when Max gave me the lift as well.

Radi was convinced that Patsy Landu saw me one night on the premises of Simon Hebe School. An entertainment activity was in session and Radi and I stood watching our former classmates through the window. Radi was worried that Patsy might share the news in her excitement, compromising my cover without realizing it. We panicked. He spoke to Patsy and she confirmed his suspicions so he warned her not to tell anyone. In addition to all this we were concerned because certain people in Mbekweni knew that I was back. In one sense this was a good thing, helping to boost morale. On the other hand, if MK supporters knew so did our enemies. This proved to be the case and I was arrested later.

In order to avoid detection we had to constantly move from place to place. I stayed with Mbulelo Grootboom, a teacher at Simon Hebe School, for two days. Mbulelo lived on the premises in a room previously used for woodworking classes that was far removed from the classrooms. During my stay Phumla Nkala and Nomhle Sithela arrived, asking for a crash course in the use of grenades. Both girls were very nervous because I used live ammunition during the demonstration. After teaching them the basics, I promised to send them to Botswana for further training. Both their boyfriends were in exile at the time and this was probably another reason they wanted to go.

Radi recommended using Makhunga Mpeluza as a courier to deliver our messages to comrades in Botswana. We briefed him about his role and he agreed without any objections, soon proving himself more than worthy.

I lived with Vivian at Garth Adam's house for a short while. One evening, walking back to Paarl East from Mbekweni, the police stopped Vivian and I on Jan van Riebeeck Road, demanding to know why we were out after dark. A curfew was in place at the time as a 'state of emergency' had been declared. Luckily, none of the policemen recognized us and we were let off with a warning. Nevertheless we called Lloyd Fortuin as soon as we arrived home, asking him to organize alternative accommodation. He contacted Anthea Sheldon and she made arrangements for me to stay with a Moslem family, the Essops, in a room overlooking their swimming pool. In case of any eventuality I was to claim that I worked for them. Mr. Essop immediately made me comfortable, asking if there was anything I needed. He and his family were extremely hospitable. Lloyd sent Vivian to a home in Wellington but the owner turned out to be a policeman. Anthea found other accommodation with Eunice and Archie Siebritz.

One evening Vivian met with his girlfriend Chantel. According to underground rules this seriously compromised security so we had to withdraw from our bases once again. Joe Patel took us to Liz Abrahams' house where we stayed for a few days. I never discussed any of our activities with her, sneaking out of the house late at night and returning before she noticed my absence.

From there, Joe Patel took us both to Cape Town. Vivian stayed with a woman named Josephine Pieterse, pretending to be a student at Western Cape University. I was taken to Observatory Station and had to wait for someone named Emily Fairbairn to pick me up. Liz told me what she would be wearing so it was easy to identify her by the scarf round her neck and other attire. Emily placed me with people in Observatory who simply knew me as a student named Themba. There were three other residents in the house including Tamara Prayer, a very friendly woman from Johannesburg who was a nurse at Groote Schuur Hospital. Tamara drove me to Sandy Beach one day, along with two of her female friends. When we arrived I could barely control my panic. Uniformed policemen patrolled a beach dotted with naked sunbathers. It was an extremely embarrassing and very nerve–wracking day.

One afternoon a bicycle disappeared from the backyard. Arriving home from work, one of the residents noticed it was missing. Tamara came to my room asking if I knew where it was but I had no idea. She threatened to call the police, putting me in a very awkward position. I said I would gladly pay for the bicycle but she turned down my offer. When the police arrived they questioned all four of us, asking where we had been during the time of the theft and when we had last seen the stolen property. Fortunately none of them recognized me and, satisfied with our statements, they left.

I worked closely with Radi Ndevu at the time, recruiting COSAS youth and sending them outside the country for training. Radi was able to move about freely and identified potential COSAS members who appeared to be loyal to the ANC. One of our de–briefing sessions took place in a bus shelter. While we sat there deep in discussion a police van drove up and did a U–turn opposite the shelter. Radi panicked and said we ought to leave straight away but I managed to dissuade him. It would look far less suspicious if we calmly continued our conversation. The plan worked admirably.

Allan Paulse and Anthea Sheldon helped Radi with his work but he had no idea they were our contacts as well. They conveyed information to and from Botswana and brought in money. In those days one was only told what one needed to know and nothing more. Now and again Vivian and I would get together, although we were only supposed to communicate by dead letter box in case one of us was arrested, tortured and forced to reveal the whereabouts of the other. Both Radi and a man named Makhunga Mpeluza helped me a great deal with the recruitment work. We also identified possible targets such as military installations and police stations in the process. I showed the recruits how to use grenades and then sent them to Botswana for training.

CHAPTER 9

My Arrest and Detainment

Ishmael Moss moved me to Gugulethu NY 134. NY was the abbreviation for Native Yard, a name given to the area during the apartheid years. A little later 'Captain' Mohlale invited me to his home for a few days before taking me to KTC where I shared a lady's house. This was an informal settlement named after the nearby Khakhaza Trading Cash store.

Vivian, Cecil Esau, Ishmael, Neville van der Rheede and myself were asked to attend a briefing session in Observatory to plan the establishment of the Western Cape MK command. The police arrested me an hour before the meeting was due to take place. If they had watched and waited a little longer we might all have suffered the same fate – or been killed. On the 17th of December 1984, four months after my return and five days before my birthday, a police officer named Madebe Manzi spotted me buying milk from a nearby shop and promptly informed the Murder and Robbery Squad. Madebe was a former schoolmate. At the time of my arrest I was on board a bus from Nyanga East terminus with twenty rand in my pocket, a key to the place where I lived and a list of secret communication codes. The bus unexpectedly came to a halt just beyond the shop where I had bought the milk a little earlier. Looking down from the upper deck I was shocked to see armed police swarming all over the place, with Officer Manzi at the forefront, leading them on. He pointed to me, whispering something to his white colleagues. Thinking quickly, I destroyed the code list, knowing I was in serious trouble.

Shouting, "We got the *terrie!*"(Afrikaans abbreviation for terrorist) they took me to Gugulethu Police Station, stripped me naked and conducted a thorough search, looking for tell–tale signs at the same time. They found them; one callous on my right shoulder from carrying an AK–47 and one on each heel caused by wearing military boots. It seemed an aeon before the security branch escorted me to a police building on Loop Street in Cape Town. Later that day Major Le Roux and Officer Kaas took me to the police cells at Stellenbosch Police Station in thumb–cuffs where I was tortured – physically and psychologically – by Le Roux and Officer Gwentu. I spent the entire night of my birthday handcuffed, standing on a small piece of tile. Every time I tried to sit down two policemen pulled me back onto my feet. By the next day I was absolutely exhausted and felt like a misused toy in some insane game. They threatened to put me into a helicopter and drop me over the sea. When Gwentu, one of my own people, started beating me I jumped onto him in wild fury and pushed him away. In one sense things could have been worse. Other comrades had been tortured with electric shocks or suffocated with rubber bags.

The photograph of Jama that the Security Branch had in their possession.

The police desperately wanted to know where we kept our arms, my present address and Vivian's whereabouts. Making use of a cover story, I told them I lived in Lady Frere and had never left the country, denying my military training. They didn't believe me so I said I had been in Lesotho. They didn't believe that either. Someone produced a photograph of Sivuyile 'Mikki' Xhayiya and Madoda Mnyamana. They had one of me as well. Mikki was with the ANC Security Branch and Madoda had been with me at Caxito camp. An informant had already told them we were MK soldiers so there was no point in denying it anymore. I finally admitted that I was trained, had recently infiltrated the country and that Vivian Matthee was responsible for organizing my accommodation at KTC. They wanted me to take them to the house where I stayed. Pretending to be unfamiliar with the area, I said I could not identify the place. Informal settlements are nothing more than a multitude of closely packed informal houses randomly erected by impoverished men and women. There were no regular streets and no sanitation or electricity. The police insisted on taking me to look for the place that night but we searched in vain so they eventually gave up. I had no intention of finding it.

The police already knew Vivian was an MK soldier and I automatically presumed he had left the country by then. Underground rules dictated that one had to disappear immediately if anything went wrong, taking all precautions in the process. Vivian and the others would have been alerted as soon as I failed to turn up for the meeting and would automatically follow proper procedures. In a case like that MK soldiers were taught to presume the worst; the missing party had either been arrested or sold out to the enemy.

After being transferred to Paarl Police Station, and hearing that Vivian had been seen in Cape Town, I tried figuring out the best way of getting a message through, telling him about my detainment and the danger he was in. If I gave the police the name of a person who could not possibly expose our network, my plan might just work. Josephine Pieterse was the only completely apolitical person I knew. She had no idea that Vivian and I were MK members and he would have left her place by then. Hopefully she would be astute enough to read between the lines and somehow pass the message on to Vivian. Sure enough, plainclothes policemen took me to her home in Athlone. They removed my handcuffs temporarily so I could speak to her without giving away what was really happening. They stuck close, pretending to be friends and hoping she would reveal Vivian's whereabouts. I knew Josephine did not know where he was.

At Paarl, guards watched over my cell twenty four hours a day in three eight–hour shifts. One of them, Wyne Durr, always sat close to the steel door of my cell with nothing but bars separating us. Privacy was an unknown luxury. I was forbidden to meet or speak with anyone. Other than issues directly related to food and health, guards were prohibited from speaking to me. Thirty minutes of exercise each day broke the tedium somewhat, plus reading permitted material. I read the Bible from Genesis to Revelation in a few days. White men issued Bibles in the mistaken belief that the scriptures would influence prisoners to become passive in their thinking. If a man slaps you on one cheek turn the other, so to speak. The Bible certainly gave me hope – and inspired me – but not in the intended manner. Instead, I perceived Jesus as a freedom fighter who came to set captives free.

Every time I tried making conversation with the guards they simply repeated that they were not allowed to speak to me. Initially Wyne was no different to his colleagues. He spent his time reading newspapers and books and I noticed that many of them were poetry books. Over time we began sharing our common interest in poetry. One day, I asked him for a pen and paper and wrote a poem about uMkhonto weSizwe, praising the liberation movement and explaining that racial divisions were caused by a system and not by skin colour. We discussed the poem and then he wrote one in Afrikaans called 'Blou Paleis' (Blue Palace – blue being the standard colour of the police service). His poem praised policemen for carrying out their duties under great difficulties. This was a wonderful breakthrough that helped to open up lines of communication. We learnt to respect one another's opposing beliefs even though we were both prepared to die for ours.

Wyne graciously complied when I asked him for newspapers. He even lent me a portable cassette player during his shifts, plus an assortment of tapes – one of them featuring Madonna. His favourite song was 'Like a Virgin'. Although the music was not to my taste it made an incredible difference, taking my mind of the reality of detention for a while. When it was cold and raining outside Wyne closed the steel gates and we were both prisoners inside the cell. I wonder if he ever gave that any thought ...

During my detention Maj. Le Roux and Officer Dantjies drove me to Cambridge Police Station in East London to correlate statements made by Madoda Mnyamana and myself and take me to the Botswanan border to identify where we had entered the country. I insisted on speaking to Madoda when we arrived but he refused to see me. Later, I learned that the security branch had recruited him over to their side. We drove to Kimberley and Col. Loots interrogated me. This was the man at the railway station who had sat reading in the Cressida when we arrived back in South Africa.

There was another shock in store for me as well. While I was in one of the offices of the security branch in Kimberley I noticed More, a black MK comrade. He had been my Military Engineering Instructor at Caxito and, as far as I knew, was detained by the Swaziland police. I had no idea he was an *askari*. More used my MK name and began to undermine the ANC; "MK soldiers are nothing more than sacrificial lambs sent off to fight while our corrupt leaders stayed at home in their comfort zones." "Joe Modise is involved in drug smuggling." "The ANC will never govern the country."

He was proud to have voluntarily betrayed that 'group of criminals' and now travelled around with the police to identify MK guerillas. According to More, one of our captured comrades, Shakes, was co–operating with them as well. He begged me to give the police my fullest co–operation because it was "time to pay the ANC back". If I did so the police would take good care of my family and me. He said he had life insurance cover. What did I have? If I died, no one would benefit.

More's latter comments shocked me but I was convinced that our cause was a just one and weighed the words of Oliver Tambo and Chris Hani against his. Tambo called this the 'Decade of Liberation' but warned us that the enemy was on the offensive. There were huge attempts to infiltrate our organization. Officials in neighbouring countries received bribes to persuade them not to allow MK members into their countries. Even so, our leaders felt sure that victory was certain.

That afternoon, More accompanied Shakes and I to the Barkley West Police Station. When we arrived he asked the black warrant officer for keys to the cells and locked us up. Shakes asked for cigarettes. More replied that he would bring them the following day. Every arrogant word and action was obviously planned to show us who was in command. So many questions came to mind. Had the entire world turned against me? Was this the same man I shared jokes with back at the camp in

Angola? How could he turn against the organization that gave so much in attempting to liberate the oppressed peoples of our country? Through-out my entire period of detention, this was by far the worst moment.

Here is the poem I wrote about this episode.

IT CAN'T BE YOU

We suffered in darkness together
We crawled through the earth together
We took up arms together
We ate every meal together
We shared accommodation together
It can't be you.

It can't be you who rejects and looks down on me
It can't be you who curses and reminds me about my poverty
It can't be you who suppresses any chance of my upward mobility
It can't be you.

It can't be you who developed trust in our adversaries more than
In your comrade of many years
It can't be you
It can't be you who belittles me and makes a mockery of my
Insignificant academic achievements
It can't be you.

I thought we were comrades
I thought I could lean on you in times of trouble
I thought I had an obligation to die for you when the need arose
Can it really be you?
Can it be you who lost our memory so easily?
It can't be you!

The police took me back to Kimberley for further interrogation the following day. They wanted to know exactly where we had entered the country and I told them that I had not been trained in reconnaissance and simply did not know. It had been pitch dark that night and we could only guess at our position.

When we reached the border Le Roux and Dantjies allowed me to climb out of the car, but I had no idea whether this was the right spot or not. They removed my handcuffs for the very first time and, for some obscure reason, took a photograph of me standing in no–man's–land between South Africa and Botswana. I was tempted to run across to the Botswanan immigration officials but quickly decided against it. That was exactly what they wanted and would give them a perfect excuse to shoot me.

Throughout the entire trip Le Roux and Dantjies kept a close watch over me. Whenever they needed a rest we stopped at a police station where I was locked in a cell until they were ready to continue with the journey. It was a long drive but I thoroughly enjoyed the fresh air and sights along the way – particularly Port Alfred, where we stayed for a few hours.

Colonel Buchner came to interrogate me when we got back to Paarl. He believed in psychological torture. Buchner had photographs of men and women who had left the country for military training, with their real names written on the back of each image. The police knew the whereabouts of some of them, the most valuable information having apparently come from Mikki Xayiya. Buchner passed me one photo at a time, told me everything they knew about that particular person and then asked me to verify the information. His strategy worked. It was useless to deny what they already knew and every time I lied he caught me out anyway. During the interrogation I found out that they had no accurate facts about Vivian's or my movements. Col. Buchner was not particularly impressed by the information I gave, saying that none of it was new. He showed me an 800–page book written in Afrikaans and apparently translated from Mikki's English version. I do not know whether he actually wrote it or not but the book included sketches of many MK military camps. Whoever drew them certainly spent time there – and knew the camps well. Of course any, or all, of the information in the book could have been compiled from the statements of other detainees, particularly if they were extracted under torture. The colonel handed me sheets of paper and told me to write down everything I knew about camp activities. There was little to write as I had not been in exile long enough to find out very much. We were only told what we needed to know and only saw what we needed to see.

Over and over again I stressed the fact that the ANC was not a violent organization. One day security forces asked me to speak to Reuben France (a COSAS member detained for burning motor vehicles) to try and persuade him to plead guilty to the charge. I agreed, so they brought him to my cell. We were excited to see one another but had very little time to speak. I quickly told him what the police expected me to achieve during our meeting. A few of the COSAS members Reuben had worked with were now safely in exile so I suggested that, rather than confessing to his crime, he put the blame on them instead.

I spent six months in isolation before being taken to the regional court in Cape Town. I thanked Wyne profusely for his friendship and kindness during my detention. We had a common bond and respected one another as human beings regardless of race, creed or colour. His words of encouragement meant such a lot. He said that he regarded me as a brother. Although there was no way of knowing whether I would be sentenced to a long imprisonment, I promised to remember what he had done for me. The day I walked out of prison a free man, I would come back and thank him again.

CHAPTER 10

My Trial

My first court appearance took place on the 14th of June 1985 with Mr. Ramesh Vassen defending. He asked for a postponement on the grounds that he needed more time to consult with me. The case was postponed until August and transferred to the Magistrate's Court in Paarl. I was moved to Pollsmoor prison to await trial. People from my hometown came to give me moral support at the court, and in prison later on. Whatever the eventual outcome, I was psychologically prepared.

Warrant Officer Nieuwoodt and Sergeant la Kay (Niewoodt's deputy) received me at Pollsmoor. I spent six months in 'A' Section where Dullah Omar and Trevor Manuel were detained. In general the prison staff treated me well, other than a single, very unpleasant experience. A warder whose name eludes me expected me to submissively jump up and run every time he called. I told him that I was not a criminal and refused to be treated as such. We ended up in an argument before a group of warders ran in and began to beat me up. They kicked me all over my body as I lay on the floor trying to protect my face – and dignity. With all the energy I had left, I punched the warder who started the fight, catching him unawares – and everything started all over again. Eventually they left me alone and called Officer Nieuwoodt who was responsible for my section. The only satisfaction I received was in finding out later that one of the warders had a very nasty cut on his lip.

On the way to the medical examination room I noticed one of my comrades, Monty Motloung, in a hospital cell. Monty had been severely tortured after his arrest along with Solomon Mahlangu – who was later hanged by the government. Motloung was psychologically unstable, very anxious and looked underfed as well. Considering the state of his health his morale was surprisingly high and he praised uMkhonto weSizwe's efforts, assuring me that the ANC would one day govern our country. He was now a 'State President's Patient'. For medical reasons he was treated as a prison patient for life and could only be released under direct written order from the State President. Once again, my resolve strengthened. It was sad seeing him caged like an animal, knowing full well that his only crime was love for his country and his people. Whenever possible I bought cigarettes and food and asked non–political prisoners to give them to him.

Trevor Manuel (presently South Africa's Minister of Finance) and Dullah Omar (our recently deceased Minister of Transport) were both members of the UDF (United Democratic Front). I was fortunate enough to speak with them and, later, the Swart family as well, who were arrested for participating in mass political campaigns spearheaded by the UDF. One day Nieuwoodt smuggled me into their communal cell where we spent time discussing politics.

As part of my daily routine I cut out relevant newspaper clippings and gave them to common law prisoners to pass on to detained comrades so they would know what was happening outside the prison. Common prisoners helped a great deal in acquiring information. They did this in exchange for money. Detainees were not allowed to buy newspapers but they could be obtained through contacts in the prison library. I gave Trevor Manuel a crash course in secret communication. This was a system we used to send clandestine messages whenever we wrote to comrades outside the prison.

One afternoon in 1985 the warders locked three dignified, robust men into cells a few meters away from mine. I made a point of arranging to get to know them as soon as possible. Sgt. la Kay gave me permission the next morning. Mzi Khumalo, Eugene Mokgoasi and Ben Fani were from Robben Island's maximum security prison, kept on the mainland because bad weather prevented the ferry from returning that day. According to them the Island was a far better penal facility than Pollsmoor. I was skeptical until their breakfast arrived. Porridge – with milk! A luxury we were not entitled to and a privilege only extended by special order from the authorities. If the magistrate sentenced me to serve a term there, things might be looking up.

Not long afterwards my lawyer, Mr. Vassen, called me to the consultation room. I passed Ahmed Kathrada, Andrew Mlangeni and Raymond Mhlaba. They were on their way to see their attorney, Priscilla Jana. Normally the warders did not allow political prisoners to come into contact with one another so it was quite a surprise. The three men were part of MK High Command, arrested for treason in 1963 and sentenced at the infamous Rivonia Trial. Other High Command members were at Pollsmoor at that stage too including Walter Sisulu and Nelson Mandela – the man who established uMkhonto weSizwe and commanded our organization.

I was fortunate enough to speak to Mandela face to face after that, while he was exercising in the courtyard behind my cell. I could hardly believe my eyes because he was normally kept in strict solitary confinement. I managed to say a few words to him through my window as he passed, introducing myself and conveying greetings from Oliver Tambo and Chris Hani. He enquired whether I knew where they were and I replied in the affirmative. They were still in exile. The brief encounter made my day. Face–to–face with our leader! I was so proud to be a soldier in this great man's army and watched him closely every time he took a walk in the courtyard after that, but we never had the opportunity of conversing again. Officers Gregory and Swart guarded him very closely. Considering what I had been through in a fraction of the time that Mandela was imprisoned made me even more determined and inspired. No matter how hard I tried after that, warders consistently refused all requests to visit the old man.

Cooks in white uniforms transported food to his cell on a trolley covered with white cloths. One day the irresistible smell of a very hearty soup wafted past my nose. I asked the men who normally dished out our food whether they could smuggle a little of it into my cell. The favour cost me. It was rich, tomato–red with pieces of chicken floating on top and tasted marvellous. What a vast difference between this and the food we were given! It was good to know that our beloved leader received decent treatment but I still complained bitterly about the poor diet the rest of us received.

On the 27th of January 1986 warders drove me to Paarl to stand trial. I prepared a speech prior to this, knowing that I would be sentenced. In it I voiced objections to being tried by an illegitimate regime, saying that I should be accorded the same status as any other soldier–at–war. Mr. Justice Lemmer presided over the courtroom and Mr. A. de Villiers la Grange was the prosecutor.

Arriving at the packed court in high spirits I saluted, shouting, *"Amandla!"* ("Power!") People responded with *"Ngawethu!"* ("It is ours!"). Dullah Omar was my defence lawyer and he advised me to plead guilty as the sentence might be more lenient. I turned his suggestion down and insisted on conducting my own defence instead. He was dead against that and asked me to give him my prepared input. After further consultation I insisted on going with a 'not guilty' plea and handed my speech over, eventually convinced that Dullah could secure a reduced sentence. He did his best and I was sentenced to seven years imprisonment on Robben Island.

People we expected to testify as witnesses for the state (More, Mnyamana and Xayiya) did not appear but Lilian, an MK comrade, did. I was speechless. Having last seen her at Caxito she had given no indication of turning *askari*. Something had taken place since then. She was very thin and would not look at me as she stood in the dock giving evidence. I smiled at her, bearing no grudge and knowing there had to be extenuating circumstances. The magistrate ordered the public to leave the gallery during her appearance. What had happened to the ANC? The rate of defection within a short time period was nothing short of astounding.

Dullah leaned over to ask whether Lilian had been in the camp with me and I answered, "Yes." Both he and the prosecutor asked why she had decided to work with the South African Police. Lilian related a story of severe suffering and abuse at the hands of certain ANC leaders. She denied having a personal grudge against myself or any other MK soldier, adding that only a few leaders were involved in the abuse.

(Due to the intense hatred that many South Africans still feel for people who assisted the apartheid regime, it would be unwise to name them. Some suffered tremendous torture before the enemy could recruit them. ANC and MK members contributed to the problem, directly or indirectly, consciously or unconsciously, by pushing many soldiers in the wrong direction, falsely accusing them of being enemy agents. I always respected the female members of uMkhonto weSizwe because they sacrificed such a great deal yet showed the same standard of competency as any other soldier. Being in the minority they were faced with the challenges of coping with pressure from male members and that alone made them vulnerable.)

After being sentenced, warders moved me to the white section at Allendale Prison where I was once again separated from my people. What a relief knowing that my isolation would only last for a single day. The next morning they handcuffed, chained and shackled me round the ankles and put me in the back of a white van with one window at the rear and small ventilators on either side. The chain made a dreadful noise so I held it up – uncomfortable yet happy, knowing I would soon be with other men of similar convictions to my own.

CHAPTER 11

Robben Island

We arrived at Table Bay harbour in Cape Town and I was placed in a holding cell on Jetty No. 1 while warders finished loading prison staff into the ferry. I could smell the sea. What would Robben Island be like? The holding cell was positioned in such a way that it was impossible to see or communicate with anyone on the outside. I had never sailed in my entire life. What would happen if the ferry sank? I knew how to swim but certainly not in handcuffs and leg–irons! It was a terrifying thought. Faith in God helped to keep me positive at that moment. Somehow, I would survive.

If memory serves me correctly, we boarded a ferry named 'Penguin' towards the end of January 1986. I was immediately taken to a small, separate compartment away from the other passengers and we soon sailed to 'The Island.'

Above the arch leading to the prison entrance was the inscription:

Welkom / Robben Eiland.
Welcome / Robben Island.
Ons dien met trots.
We serve with pride.

ROBBEN ISLAND

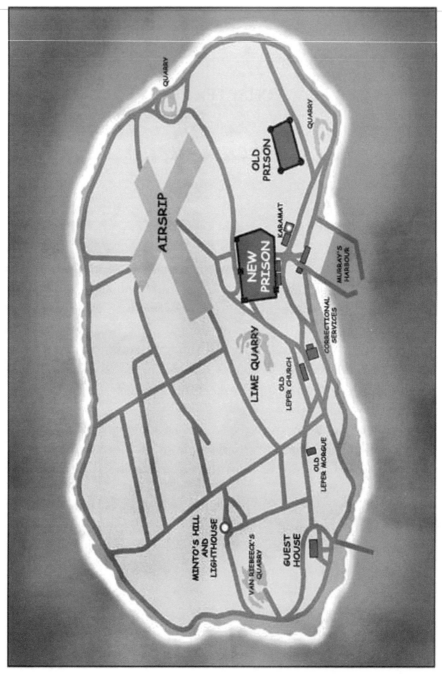

ROBBEN ISLAND PRISON

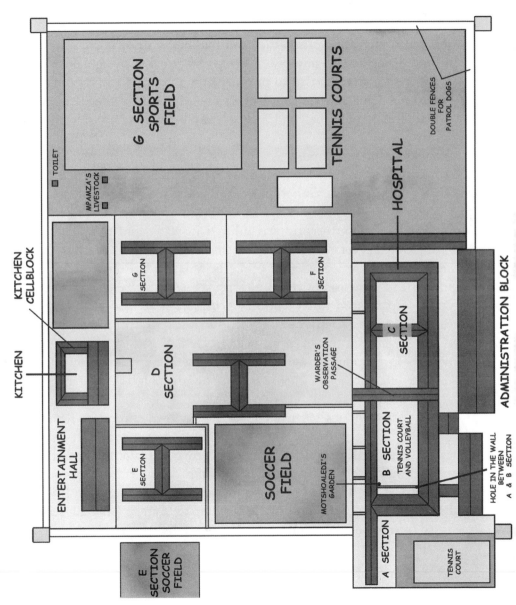

At the beginning of every year, officials allocated a number to each new prisoner, starting with one. Warders addressed us by these numbers. As I was the first prisoner to arrive that year, my new name became '1/86'. A warder issued me with a prison card and told me to strip. There was no point in resisting and, in any case, I was getting used to being naked by now, although it never ceased to be a degrading exercise. I handed over my treasured Citizen watch and belt. These meagre personal items were placed in a moneybag and locked away before I received a 'new' uniform.

Robben Island's maximum security prison consists of nine sections – cell sections 'A' to 'G', the kitchen and the hospital. Sgt. Matthee led me to 'C' Section, issued a sanitation bucket, Jeyes antiseptic fluid, toilet paper, wash rags, soap, toothpaste, toothbrush and pyjamas and then locked me in. The antiseptic was diluted in water and poured into the sanitation bucket to neutralize smells. Prisoners used the buckets at night after being locked up. 'C' is the smallest prison section on Robben Island. The warder could not speak English so we conversed in Afrikaans. Apart from thirty minutes exercise a day I was alone until Zamile Mazantsana from Port Elizabeth arrived. Sfiso Buthelezi from KwaZulu Natal, Bushy Maape from the North West and others were brought to 'C' Section later on as well. Bushy, a former school principal, was escorted in barefoot as a severe form of humiliation but we managed to laugh about it afterwards.

It was a tremendous relief not to be on my own any more. Before they arrived there was no one to speak to other than Ntshebe Magxwalisa, the MK prisoner who brought my meals, and the few prisoners who walked between the various sections during exercise periods. Fortunately Ntshebe relayed messages for me as well, to and from ANC leaders. In this way I found out that certain of our people had been recruited by other organizations and others were discrediting the ANC.

As the number of prisoners in our section gradually increased over the next month, warders transferred us to 'A' Section. It was a bit bigger and had a tennis court and space to play table tennis. Although I never wished for a friend to be caught and imprisoned, I was nevertheless very excited when Radi arrived. As we both came from the same township I knew he could fill me in with all the latest developments. We talked about fellow comrades who were still at large or in exile, especially Patrick, the leader of our unit who played such a major role in Paarl politics and the armed struggle.

Radi and I spoke about the deaths of Norman and Vivian – our close friends and coloured comrades who made such a tremendous contribution to the struggle. Neither of them sought glory but totally committed themselves to destroying apartheid. I was in their unit when we left the country. Quiet, disciplined and action–orientated, Vivian was in his final year of studying towards a law degree at the University of the Western Cape when he died. The people in his township loved and respected him and he was an excellent scrumhalf who excelled at rugby – a member of 'Izibane' (Highlights). If Vivian were still alive today, I have no doubt that he would have been accepted to play for the Springboks.

Unlike Vivian, who is buried at a 'Hero's Acre', Norman lies in an ignominious grave unbefitting his stature. Apartheid security forces brutally murdered him at his home in KTC informal settlement in Gugulethu.

At first, what irritated me most on Robben Island was being forced to listen to classical music in the evenings. I hated that sort of music and honestly thought it was a subtle form of torture inflicted by prison authorities. In actual fact they gave each prisoner a chance to choose his favourite music on a rotation basis. The Sports and Recreation Committee distributed a book listing all the available records. Warders played them over a loudspeaker system so that everyone could hear. Prison authorities kept the money that we received from friends and family and we were allowed to ask visitors to buy records for us and bring in when they came. I purchased one that I was crazy about at the time, 'For the Sake of Love' by Isaac Hayes, and slowly learnt to appreciate classical music as well.

A favourite therapy involved viewing one another's photograph albums, identifying people we saw when they came for a visit. The albums had beautiful covers. Robben Island had its share of talented artists, who decorated the covers for us. Some of the men who owned water–colour paints and drawing pads showed us how to make our own greeting cards. The technique was very simple. After placing a mask of some sort over the paper first, we dipped the bristles of an old toothbrush into paint and then brushed it against the teeth of a comb.

Tiny particles of paint sprayed onto the paper surface and a shape became visible when we removed the mask. Once the paint had dried, the finished product looked every bit as good as a shop–bought product.

Pictures of women always elicited interesting inquiries from the owner of the album. It would not always end there. Some of the men went a step further, writing to the girls and occasionally conducting long–distance love affairs. We wanted little more than to lead a normal, stable family life. Unfortunately for some, many love affairs ended on the day of their release. Others rushed into marriage but few of these unions lasted. Many of us gave small gifts to people who visited us as well, in appreciation of their support. We ordered Parker pens from the tuck shop, inscribed the name of the intended beneficiary onto the barrel and then rubbed white correction fluid into the carved characters.

We all loved tea and coffee, regardless of the weather, and called the beverages 'umjovo', the Zulu word for injection. Some of us were so addicted that, prior to exercising our thinking abilities, we simply had to have our umjovo. Fresh water was at a premium. Rain storage tanks were situated under the gutter pipes outside our section but were badly maintained, so the water was normally dirty. Bodies and clothing were washed in salty, brackish water as no fresh water was available from the Island's taps. Bathing in it made our skin dry and flaky. Men with sensitive skins organized a letter from the doctor, exempting them from bathing in brackish water. The rest of us neutralized the dehydrating minerals by applying Colgate shampoo all over our bodies instead of soap and it genuinely worked. After rinsing, we rubbed in Nivea body lotion. I cannot tell you who came up with that solution because I never bothered to ask.

Every cell had a small two–way intercom speaker, allowing prisoners to listen to the radio and communicate with warders in the evenings if there was a problem. But – there was one big drawback. Warders controlled the volume from the censor office, making it very difficult for men who were busy studying. Eventually, someone developed a solution to this problem as well. We took a piece of floor mat, old blanket or toilet paper, stuffed it inside a small, rectangular cardboard box and placed it over the intercom to deaden the sound.

We were ordinary human beings and tempers could run high at

times. James Mange had a small cat that he called '*Sibisibi*'. He loved it passionately and really looked after it well. An unfortunate incident occurred when Stephen 'Rider' Nkebe accidentally stood on the cat, killing it instantly. James was dreadfully upset and became very angry so we all gave him moral support through his time of grief. He knelt down and gently laid *Sibisibi* in a small grave that he dug outside 'D' Section cells, refusing to speak to Rider after that.

The prison administrators transferred our group to 'D' Section towards the middle of my first year, to cells previously occupied by SWAPO prisoners. At the time, South West Africa (now Namibia) was under South African administration. These prisoners had been sent back home when the time for independence drew near.

I became part of the ANC Section Command structure together with Sfiso, Bushy and, later on, Jeff Radebe (currently Minister of Public Enterprises). Sfiso gave me the nickname *Siphithi–phithi*, which means confusion. Some of the prisoners thought it referred to my prowess on the soccer field but the name was actually used to describe me as one who got involved in everything – but left a lot unfinished. I played soccer, rugby, tennis, volleyball and athletics, every musical instrument that was available to us and took part in all the indoor games as well.

We accepted the fact that we were prisoners and made the best of each day. Fridays were the worst. Warders distributed the mail on Fridays and those who did not receive any letters felt terribly depressed. I treated mine with great respect, not reading them until we were locked up for the night. I used to take a shower in the communal ablution room, put on clean pyjamas and climb into bed, opening the letter very slowly and gently and reading it over and over again, analyzing each sentence and smiling endlessly if it contained good news. Sfiso's bed was right next to mine so he teased me mercilessly throughout the entire ritual.

In an attempt to lighten the atmosphere on Fridays we cracked jokes, saying that if one was not a good lover outside prison, one should not expect miracles. Girlfriends would not suddenly write simply because we were inside. Not everyone took the jokes lightly. Some men would not speak to persecutors for days on end. After a suitable period had passed, friends would try to discourage them from sulking. Occasionally, the reason for one's bad mood was blamed on *udliwa yijele* (the frustrations of living in prison). Understanding that there might be problems in a prisoner's family or love life as well, we respected one another's mood to a certain degree but it became the subject of a joke sooner or later. PAC and BCM comrades would pull our legs now and again, especially when we received no letters from home. They attacked us left and right, cracking jokes or pretending to sympathize. We were like one big family, more or less the same age, forgetting our different political affiliations for a while. We respected one another and did our best to resolve problems that threatened to create division.

The authorities knew how much we valued written correspondence but that did not stop them from censoring our letters. By the time they finished cutting portions out, we were sometimes left with nothing more than disjointed words on bits of stapled paper. The amounts differed from letter to letter. In some cases the recipient (in prison and at home) could more or less understand what had been written but, in others, it was virtually impossible to make out anything at all. We often blamed the Censor Office for causing irreparable breakdowns in families and marriages. They removed important information and censored the mail in such a way that remaining words meant something entirely different to the original. They violated our human rights. Neither writer nor recipient was in a position to immediately explain the misunderstanding so disputes often arose, psychologically destroying prisoners and relationships. Nevertheless, it was better to get an over–censored letter than none at all.

The length of a prisoner's outgoing letter was important as well. I spent a lot of time writing letters – a first draft of up to fifteen pages before editing it down to the permitted word count. My friends teased me, asking whether I was busy with a thesis. I cannot recall exactly how many words were regarded as making up one letter. Censor Officers counted our words and if one was not careful, a single letter could end up being classified as two or more – reducing one's letter quota. If the quota was used up, one could convert unused visiting time to make up the deficit. Our external lives were virtually in the hands of the Censor Officers. They were only too willing to use their authority to punish prisoners, denying them news, warmth and love.

It was the same when it came to visits. Warders enjoyed telling us when our thirty minutes were over. Parting was very difficult, especially as we had a limited number of visits per year. 'D Group' prisoners were allowed twelve thirty–minute visits per year. All prisoners longed for some demonstration of love and support from family and friends, expecting to receive at least one visitor per allotted date. It was a tremendous disappointment if they failed to arrive. Warders cruelly rubbed it in by sneering, *"Jou besoeker het nie opgedaag nie!"* ("Your visitor hasn't pitched up!") The disappointed prisoner always felt as if his family and friends simply did not care enough to even bother. Of course, he found out the reason for their absence later on but it never helped, no matter how genuine the excuse. We craved exterior communication.

We accommodated as many visitors as possible to keep our morale high. To emphasize the importance of regular communication, friends did everything they could to encourage people on the outside to write to men who received no letters from home, or to visit lonely prisoners. They even went to the effort of organizing girlfriends and asking their visitors to relay messages for their friends.

It was such a delight to see their happy faces when they arrived, but it was so painful saying goodbye. The visitor's block is adjacent to the prison arch and about 100 metres from Murray's harbour. We stood behind the arch, waving as our loved ones walked back to the ferry. Sadly, some of them did not know whether to respond or not, being nervously unsure of prison procedure. Afterwards, we slowly moved off in small, thoughtful groups as warders escorted us approximately 300 metres back to prison like a flock of sheep. Sometimes visitors brought good news and sometimes they brought bad news. The latter made us feel terribly guilty. We were unable to play our part in solving family problems or issues relating to politics, but one eventually learned to accept these restrictions.

I recall one particular incident when Zamile Mazantsana caught sight of his mother at Table Bay harbour on the mainland. She was on her way to pay him a surprise visit but he was being taken to hospital in a prison van. Zamile shouted out at the top of his voice calling, *"Molo, mama!"* ("Hello, mother!") She yelled back, *"Molo, mtwana wam!"* ("Hello, my child!"). She could not see him but recognized her beloved son's voice. For days afterwards, this incident was all he could speak about.

In 1986 all prisoners from 'D' Section participated in a hunger strike against poor prison conditions and later joined by 'F' Section. This was a very clear indication of the unity we shared. PAC and BCM members joined the ANC, never once claiming that any particular party had initiated it.

On Fridays we ate supper very early (at 3 pm) so we kept our food until later. At times, prisoners from other sections gave us extra bread, particularly the men from 'G' Section, as some of them were classified as 'A Group'. Prisoners in this group were allowed to buy certain items from the tuck shop – radios, newspapers, groceries, etc. – and had the highest visit and letter quotas. In addition to this, warders permitted them physical contact with visitors. 'B Group' prisoners could buy groceries as well but received less letters and visits than 'A Group'. 'C Group' could purchase the same items as 'D Group' but enjoyed fewer visits and letters than 'B Group'. 'D Group' prisoners, the lowest in rank, could only purchase items such as toiletries, shoe polish and cigarettes and our quota was the least. We swapped some of these items with other groups in exchange for food and even managed to smuggle in a hot plate that we hid away whenever someone tipped us off about a pending search. To a certain degree after that, we ate a better variety of food and could warm it up as well. Our section clubbed together in a communal style of living that we called *Kolkhos* (Collective), sharing whatever we could.

Although we made the best of a bad situation, certain issues still needed to be challenged. We could not understand why the authorities treated us differently to the other political prisoners and, refusing to be regarded as common criminals, decided to embark on a hunger strike. Other sections joined in later, except the ANC leadership in 'B' Section who opposed the strike. We exempted men suffering from diabetes, ulcers and other illnesses from participating.

This is a list of our grievances:
- Censoring of letters
- Censoring of videocassettes
- Prisoner classification system

- System of application regarding visitors
- System of application regarding letters
- Shackling of patients taken to hospital on the mainland
- Using a small, closed van for transporting patients to hospital
- Keeping prisoners below deck on the ferry
- Restricted diet
- Restriction of sports activities
- Restriction of sportswear
- Prohibition of musical instruments
- Lack of telephone booths
- Restriction of physical contact with visitors
- Prohibition of television sets in communal cells
- Restricted access to other prison sections

The warders permitted our section leaders – Sfiso, Bushy and myself – as per ANC leadership instruction to meet in the study room with Govan Mbeki and Wilton Mkwayi, senior ANC leaders from 'B' Section. We listed our grievances but they insisted on confining the meeting to the issue of food. Mbeki told us that Robben Island had a long history. Early prisoners lived on a diet of maize but eventually received bread. They slept on mats on the bare floor but were later given beds. He therefore advised us to take things slowly and call off the strike. Mbeki and Mkwayi undertook to supply us with bread and we asked how long they planned to do this for. They deliberately avoided the question, placing emphasis on the fact that grievances could not be resolved in a single day. Robben Island Prison had changed tremendously since the sixties. We all knew the horror stories – warders urinating in prisoners' mouths or burying them up to their necks in sand as punishment for minor offences. Nevertheless, none of us felt happy about their advice, convinced we were on the right track, but we had to obey their instruction.

Many older prisoners who had been on the island from as early as the sixties ridiculed the whole exercise, accusing us of being hot–blooded and impulsive and insisting that the authorities would not rectify our grievances, given the nature of penal systems. *"Bane D-D-D"*, they added. (This meant that we still suffered from detention hangover).

Judges sent us to prison because they saw us as criminals who could never exercise rational judgment.

On the other hand, we believed that men kept behind bars for too long accepted defeat and no longer had the motivation to challenge prison authority. They grew increasingly submissive and we did not intend to follow suit. Interestingly enough, after the prison administration addressed and rectified some of the grievances, these men benefited along with the rest of us but never once praised our 'impossible' achievements.

Michael Gqamane and I collapsed after nine days and landed up in the hospital section. Our comrades appealed to us to eat because we were so weak by then. We both rejected their entreaties but drank a hot solution of water, salt and sugar instead. That night, unable to pull myself onto the bed, I slept on the floor.

Two remarkably energetic BCM members showed no signs of wilting, obviously eating on the sly. Evidence backed up our suspicions but we decided not to make an issue out of it.

After the strike, warders permitted other sections to play tennis at 'G' Section. This was a great victory. The authorities made additional concessions too, such as allowing electrical musical instruments into the prison and team sport activities with other sections. They also gave us permission to wear tracksuits on sports days. At first we followed the latter privilege to the letter but, after a few weeks, wore them whenever we wanted. They reacted negatively but relaxed the rules as time went by. Led by Tokyo Sexwale, constant pressure from our Sports and Recreation Committee helped the process along nicely.

Thanks to our hunger strike, television was introduced into the prison. South Africa's first broadcasts began on January the 6th 1976 so many older prisoners had never seen TV before. When the weather was cold, prisoners arrived at the communal cells wrapped warmly in grey prison blankets, kept in place with Baba Mdlalose's homemade safety pins – all looking like Basotho tribesmen. We watched our heroes and heroines, especially the South Africans. Had it not been for apartheid, our talented African, Indian and Coloured sportsmen might have appeared on television back then as well.

Brenda Fassie was the most popular singer and we all called her

'Mabree'. We appreciated the contribution of all local stars especially Miriam Makeba, Letta Mbuli, Caiphus Semenya and Jonas Gwangwa. Most of us loved the music of Luther Vandross, Barry White, Shirley Bassey, Mozart, Barbara Streisand, Diana Ross, Bob Marley, Rodney Winston and Teddy Pendergrass. Their music penetrated deep into our hearts and helped to fill a part of the ever–present gap in our lives – wanting to be with family and friends again. We played videocassettes as well, including one that featured Diana Ross and Rodney Winston 'Live in Paris', and we recorded different artists from a television programme called *Ingxubevange* (a mixture of things).

In particular, every one of us treasured the artists who supported Amnesty International and The International Red Cross. Mere words fail to express how much we valued their contribution – reminding the world that people like us were still in prison because of our political beliefs. Sting, Bruce Springstein, Tracy Chapman, Jonas Gwangwa, the ANC Cultural Group and many more – thank you so much. You consoled so many of us, providing love, care and inspiration.

Television caused its share of problems too. One laughable incident involved two short–tempered prisoners who both wanted to watch different programmes at the same time. One stood up and switched to his channel. On his way back to bed, the other one walked over and changed to the channel he wanted to view. They both ended up in front of the television, frantically switching from one channel to the other. Sfiso occupied the same cell at the time so he switched the television off completely, complaining that he was sick and tired of their nonsense.

I met many interesting characters while on Robben Island and my story would not be complete if I failed to mention a few of them.

On the whole, most of the prisoners sentenced after 1986 were young, energetic radicals who demanded immediate transformation. Soon, a new group of militants arrived including Derrick McBride, Vincent James (a hardliner), Dr Veejay Ramlakan, Dr Sibongiseni Dhlomo, Gordon Webster and Allen Pearce. Prison authorities labeled Derrick McBride a rebel when he complained about the lack of effort put into saving his son Robert from the gallows in Pretoria. He demanded to be imprisoned with his son and refused to settle for anything less.

Harry Gwala was imprisoned on the island too. A group of us visited him at the hospital section where he lay ill at the time. Harry hated white people, regarding them all as the enemy. Adamant that there could never be any form of reconciliation with these oppressors, he believed the only language they understood was 'the barrel of a gun'.

Joseph Makhura and Weaver arrived later on. Joseph, a medical officer at Viana at one stage, is a very softhearted comrade whose discipline is remarkable – an MK member the ANC can truly be proud of. Weaver was the soldier whom the Camp Commander tied to a tree at Caxito but we forgot our differences and became friends.

I met Ruth and Sizakele's father, Truman Matobako and spoke to him with no feelings of guilt, telling him how strong his daughters were and that they were in capable hands now, convinced that my decision to protect Ruth from further abuse had been the right thing to do.

Dingaan Mdlalose, also known as Disco, was previously imprisoned at Quattro in Angola where security officials beat him up for smoking dagga and then released him to fight in South Africa. Security forces arrested and tortured him before the court sentenced him to Robben Island. Like many other MK soldiers, Disco admitted there were times when he came close to having a nervous breakdown but Oliver Tambo's stirring words always came to mind, helping him endure the pain. Mikki, the man responsible for imprisoning him (and other soldiers in Angola) spoke about his feelings too, confessing his discomfort at being imprisoned with those same men.

After being transferred to 'F' Section, I met Nceba Faku (the current Mayor of Nelson Mandela Metropole [previously Port Elizabeth]) and David Moisi from Sebokeng, commonly known as 'Speech'.

A hard worker and health–conscious sports fanatic, Nceba was always in a good mood and very fond of analyzing everything, including censored letters that recipients were unable to decipher. In addition, he always kept the tea urn filled with water and cleaned our toilets and cells when the rest of us were sent to work at a place called *Bougroep* (Building Group) – a skills–development centre about one kilometre from the prison where I was taught bricklaying.

Nceba, popularly known as 'Giraffe' because of his height, hammered us for lowering the standards of cleanliness, insisting that we act responsibly. Whenever we held any sort of meeting he never failed to raise this particular issue.

A comrade appropriately nicknamed 'Drama' had a very short temper. Whenever he was upset, he would invite the person who offended him to a physical confrontation. Although I witnessed many of these challenges, I never actually saw him engaged in a fight. David possessed an analytical mind and was a great admirer of English literature, randomly dropping heavy English words and phrases into IsiZulu or IsiXhosa conversations. One needed to consult a dictionary in order to understand what he was talking about. He told us what it was like on death row. The courts had sentenced him to death but later commuted it to life imprisonment. To relieve stress, David learned to play the saxophone as part of his informal musical studies and also took a BA degree in prison, majoring in English and the theory of literature. He hung a grey prison blanket beside his bed to hide the fact that he studied during the day. This was prohibited as we were only allowed to study in the evenings and the privilege could be taken away for any infringement. Fortunately warders did not connect the blanket to anything more than his need for privacy. David and I greeted each other by raising an index finger and saying "The very last!" – referring to Oliver Tambo's statement that the national election due to take place sometime in 1988 would be the last white election. This statement had a profound impact, convincing us that it was just a matter of time before South Africa was in the hands of the majority.

Justice Mpanza raised chickens, rabbits, and ducks. The meat he provided on an ad–hoc basis made a huge difference to our diet. At times, prisoners stole and slaughtered one or two rabbits without his permission, roasting them at the back of 'F' section. This drove the poor man crazy and he used to stand outside yelling at the top of his voice that the men were ill disciplined and inconsiderate. After Justice left prison, Naphtali Manana took over the very important work of providing us with alternative food, especially on days when sub–standard meals were served.

Baba Mdlalose, our safety pin manufacturer, made especially soft, warm shoes as well. He was an old man and typical father figure who took it upon himself to look after the younger men. It is interesting to note how he came to be in prison in the first place. The police arrested his closest friend, Mathews Meyiwa. Meyiwa refused to leave Baba behind, admitting to the police that they worked together. Equally determined not to be separated from Mathews, Baba confirmed his friend's statement. They were both sentenced to long–term imprisonment. The two men joked about this, insisting that it was not an act of betrayal but one of solidarity and true comradeship.

Zondo, an aged prisoner whom we all called '*Mkhulu*' (old man), came from a rural area in Kwazulu Natal. His only crime had been in giving shelter to MK cadres. An *Induna* (headman) who had no political affiliations and no idea that he was harbouring MK soldiers, Mkhulu acted out of *ubuntu* (humility and concern), a mistake he was not to forget for a long time. About eighty years old when I met him, he constantly missed the company of women and kept 'girlie' magazines hidden under his mattress. Whenever we taught Mkhulu politics, he was extremely interested and eager to learn. He was released somewhat earlier than expected, due to illness. Although prisoners were deprived of female company, some of them for many years, homosexuality was regarded as a weakness among black men. As far as I know, no incidents of this nature took place, as we lived in communal cells. However, a few rumours did circulate but there was never any evidence to back them up.

I was surprised to meet Mr. Bogatsu, sentenced to imprisonment on the Island sometime between 1987 and 1988, and recognized him immediately. He was the old man who drove us from the border to Kimberley when we infiltrated South Africa. After introducing myself, he had no difficulty in recognizing me either. Bogatsu was a citizen of Botswana who was involved in ANC activities. Apparently he kept on helping them until his subsequent arrest, ending up in the same prison as many of the men he assisted. Weak and ill by the time he arrived, Bogatsu's health deteriorated even further.

'Bra' Ray entertained us with his jokes. His job involved distributing cleaning material and clothing. Whenever one spoke to him, one always ended up laughing. He helped to lessen tensions and kept us occupied with his highly amusing stories. In my opinion, he would have made a great film actor had he pursued that particular career. One day Bra exchanged words with Dime Kekana (known as *Skorokoro*), an entertainer in his own right. They moved up close, belly–to–belly and ready to fight. I cannot remember how the argument started but they never got round to finishing it. Bra Ray had Dime doubled over with laughter when he said, *"Die lytie kom hier by my met so 'n klein pens!"* ("This little boy comes to me with such a small belly!")

At one stage a coloured man from Uitenhage, sentenced to serve three years imprisonment (whom we only knew as 'Gadaffi') arrived under very mysterious circumstances. Simon Phumolang Leholo from George, nicknamed 'Castro', reported to the ANC structures that this man was an informer working for the security police. This created quite a panic and they duly reported the matter to Dullah Omar. The coloured fellow disappeared after a time – as mysteriously as he arrived. Someone said he had been released but no one knew his whereabouts after he left. It was obvious that enemy agents desperately wanted to infiltrate the prison, if that had not happened already. The incident taught us to be extra vigilant. Obviously, being a prisoner on Robben Island did not necessarily indicate one's loyalty. In my personal opinion what one did before, during and after imprisonment gives a far more balanced picture of one's commitment. Certain individuals used incarceration as a 'card' to glory and popularity.

So many comrades helped to turn the prison into a home and educational facility in one way or another, shaping the lives of many and producing prospective leaders. I really appreciated their caring, camaraderie and unselfishness. Had it not been for the efforts of these very special men, serving a sentence on Robben Island would have been sheer hell.

To while away the time we rehearsed music and lyrics from songs we sang back in the camps. By this time, instruments were allowed. Rehearsals took place in the toilet and were spontaneous and creative. I played the 'drum' (a spoon and metal plate) at first and then learned the guitar, eventually forming my own African rhythm band called *'Senzeni'* (What have we done?), along with Tebogo, Mike Mbatha from KwaZulu Natal, Jongumzi Sisulu, 'Blacks' Joyi from Langa in Cape Town and Weaver. I never studied music but managed to arrange the lyrics and music, telling the band members what I needed. From there, we rehearsed until we got it right. I experimented with the flute, guitar, violin and saxophone and sang and played drums and congas on certain occasions. One particular song that I composed warned P.W. Botha that our country was in danger. Sipho Madondo played the soprano sax and Patrick Mogale from Limpompo Province sang with me.

Sipho 'Ronnie' Mabena and I were at Caxito Camp together before he was promoted to Camp Commissar at Viana. We played on Robben Island for a group called 'Roots' that included Thabane Zulu, 'Lucky' Maphumulo, Curtis Mhlanzi and 'Shuffle' Jwarha. Ronnie and Shuffle composed the songs. In December, different groups put on performances and played a wide range of music from classic to ballads. We organized poetry readings, choirs, gumboot and other traditional dances – in fact, any type of entertainment we could come up with. I wrote poetry but always asked someone else to read my work, especially Afrika Hlapo who was really good at recital.

One of our biggest social events took place in the hall on the 5th of January 1990 – The Summer Games Awards – and covered a wide variety of indoor and outdoor sports activities. Various clubs from different sections attended. Those who excelled were rewarded for their dedication and hard work. As General Secretary, Tokyo Sexwale presented medals bought on the mainland. I received a gold medal and certificate in the rugby division. It was a joyful occasion that reminded me of the 'outside' world and, just for a moment, made me feel like a free man. The gold medal for soccer went to Lungisani Kunene from KwaZulu Natal. Andile Hewukile from Mdantsane in East London received the tennis medal and the athletics award went to Jabulani Ngobese from Gauteng. All the medals had our names engraved on them. If the event had been televised, viewers would have been quite sure that prisoners were treated as kings. Our Sports and Recreation Committee put on an exceptional meal and purchased cakes from the mainland. They organized microphones, speakers, electric guitars, drums, congas, saxophones, a keyboard, clarinet and flute. Tables were beautifully decorated, seating arrangements properly organized and the stage looked superb. That was definitely the highlight of my stay on Robben Island. Many of us forgot we were prisoners for a short while and regarded ourselves as part of the wider community. It is therefore appropriate for me to extend my greatest appreciation to the committee members. They took an entire year to organize the event with blood, sweat and tears.

In between social events, prisoners were permitted to study with outside institutions that offered lessons by correspondence, such as UNISA (University of South Africa).

Robben Island's political prisoners were the most vocal group in the country because we had the advantage of being incarcerated along with our leaders. During lunchtimes, and in the afternoons, we held clandestine political classes called 'umrabulo' (drinking), meaning that we drank from the political wisdom of other comrades and selected political literature. Different people took turns leading the discussions. Strategically placed lookouts kept us informed of any imminent searches. This responsibility was assigned to comrades who were also entrusted with safeguarding our literature. Banned books, including 'Man and his country' by Govan Mbeki and other material used during discussions, would quickly be wrapped in plastic, buried safely in the soil behind the cell and exhumed the following day.

Teaching gave me great pleasure. Most political prisoners were fluent in English and able to tackle political science–related topics without a problem. A few had left school too early so I helped them with Mathematics and Biology, although these were subjects that I hated at school. Africa Hlapo had no problem writing, speaking, or reading English but he wrote very slowly. This put him at a disadvantage, especially when he was placed with other students and given the same time limit to complete a task. Africa never spoke about his problem but I soon detected it.

We now enjoyed interaction with comrades at 'B' section, unlike before the hunger strike. We discussed politics with men like Tokyo Sexwale, Naledi Tsiki and Peter–Paul Ngwenya, and counted ourselves privileged. They played a big role in communicating the views and thoughts of the ANC leaders and, as a direct result, we came to understand their convictions.

We listened to Elias Motsoaledi's words of wisdom as well. He spent a lot of time in the garden at the boundary of 'B' Section. Before lunch, he always cleaned out a furrow used to channel water from 'B' Section through a small hole in the wall that divided it from 'A' Section.

Prisoners in 'A' Section smuggled documents through the hole that we read and discussed while the warders were at lunch.

By this time, we were also permitted to negotiate with warders for permission to sleep in different Sections over weekends, returning to our own cells on Sundays. A few prisoners practiced what we called 'ukuphetshezela' (a disappearing act), and went to other Sections during lunchtime without permission, even though ANC leaders discouraged them. Denmark Tungwana, an ukuphetshezela specialist, argued that he only had a short sentence to serve and wanted to get as much information as possible from the men in 'B' Section. He is currently the Deputy Director of Robben Island.

As always, sport played a big part in my life. Two particular events that I participated in on the Island continue to stick in my mind. In the first, I ran in a five thousand–metre race and came third. Two great athletes beat me to the finish line, Simon Ngcime – a PAC and APLA (Azanian People's Liberation Army) member from Paarl (who, incidentally, was inspired by me to first take part in the struggle) – and Jabulani Ngobese, currently working for the Reserve Bank. A metre from the end, my legs could not carry me another step and I almost gave up until I heard Sfiso and the others cheering. Taking a dive, I managed to hurl myself across the finish line.

The second event took place when we played competition soccer against a stronger team from 'E' Section. At halftime the score was three–nil in their favour. We desperately needed to win this game. I managed to score three goals to equalize. Sfiso scored two more goals, bringing the final tally up to five–all. Sfiso was responsible for physical training in preparation for the match and took his job very seriously indeed. Some of us tried evading the rigorous training exercises but he searched all the cells until he found us. It was like being put through military training all over again. A few team members faked illness. Others excused themselves when it rained but Sfiso would firmly say, "There is no rain in the army!" Sport is fun and entertaining but it can be dangerous as well. One or two players broke legs during particularly rough tackles. We enjoyed dramatizing their injuries, taking the injured parties off the field in a wheelbarrow because we had no stretchers.

World sporting events captivated everyone's attention, particularly rugby, soccer and tennis tournaments. We sat glued to the television screen when females played netball and tennis and called this 'amayeza' (medicine), getting wildly excited when they jumped up in their short skirts and we caught a glimpse of feminine underwear.

During the tennis season, great numbers of prisoners waited their turn to play on the tennis court. The same thing happened during the soccer season. We even named certain comrades after famous football players like Maradonna and Ruud Gulliet. We also had teams of *amarhawu* (amateurs) – highly entertaining soccer players who had no idea what they were doing. Some of them suffered injuries due to lack of know–how, tackling one another and literally wrestling over the ball. They were great fun to watch and gained the most supporters. Over time, a few managed to improve a great deal.

After some time I left 'F' Section, when the authorities transferred me to the kitchen where we slept in our own cells. It was here that I met Sipho Madondo and Petrus Mashego. Madondo took charge of the kitchen and was an accomplished soprano saxophonist. Always neat, calm and highly disciplined, he was perfect for the task. An uncompromising Marxist who, together with 'Speech', once faced death by hanging (this was later commuted to life imprisonment). Petrus took extra *umrabulo* (political classes) with me. We analyzed and discussed Marxism and he contributed immensely in helping me to train my analytical skills. Although just as stubborn and short–tempered as his friend 'Speech', Petrus loved his work, providing milk for prisoners with medical prescriptions and taking great pains in the preparation procedures. Mashego never exercised but played an exceptional game of soccer. How he stayed fit was a total mystery. A punctual and unusually precise person, he clarified every sentence uttered to him in conversation, making quite sure that he understood correctly.

Somewhere around 1988 or 1989 my throat became increasingly sore. A medical officer diagnosed the problem as tonsillitis and organized for them to be removed at City Park Private Hospital in Cape Town, where I stayed for two days. Guards kept me under constant surveillance and chained my leg to the bed. It was uncomfortable but I enjoyed being away from prison. It would have been nice to have stayed a while longer.

In general, we all got on very well with men from other political affiliations, although issues occasionally cropped up that had to be resolved. Fortunately they were seldom of a serious nature. The subject matter of our jokes knew no boundaries. Comrades made comments about our various struggles and organizations, some of them very insensitive. Under normal circumstances we would have reacted with real anger, possibly resorting to fistfights as well. We never experienced that in our Section. In fact, prisoner maturity was quite remarkable.

Inevitably we were also subject to jailers who had really bad attitudes – and vice versa. Afrika Hlapo's temper was legendary by now. He came very close to spending time in solitary confinement a few times after beating up warders who upset him. On one occasion Afrika threatened to stop eating altogether if they put him in a cell on his own again. He was left alone after that.

While I was working in the kitchen a new warder named Smit arrived, who was extremely outspoken when it came to his right wing views. He tried to be difficult but, thankfully, it didn't take long to tame this 'raging lion'. We went out of our way to demonstrate a high level of maturity and he soon realized the huge difference between political and criminal prisoners.

Sister Gericka was everyone's favourite staff member, a tall, polite, and very gentle nurse. Whenever one of us had a medical query and she was on duty, we prayed for her to be the one to attend us. She always treated her patients with respect and was exceptionally good at her job.

Relationships between prisoners and warders differed from one person to another but were pretty good, on the whole. It was important to develop good relationships in order to obtain favours, and persuade warders to help with a little smuggling. Some of them were sympathetic to our cause while others were not. A few chose to stick to their jobs and not get involved in political discussions. Strangely enough, certain warders held the ANC leaders, especially Nelson Mandela, in high regard.

At that time Farieda was in Pollsmoor Prison on the mainland. Here are a few words she wrote about her experience:

It is now June 1989, when Cape Town winters show no mercy. Rain, wind, snow – all in one day. I sit in my four–by–four cell at Pollsmoor

Prison and wonder about the prisoners across the sea. Jama is one of the many I know are on Robben Island. They keep each other company. I am all alone. The minutes and hours tick by and I am forced to occupy my days as best as possible so I don't have to think too much.

Even so, winters are worse in a big, cold cell on an island. The sun is good to me. In the afternoon it will visit my cell, shine onto my bed and move slowly on. It brings a little bit of added warmth. I have blankets and can keep my blood from freezing by doing a few exercises in my cell. It was too cold to go outside during exercise time and enjoy some fresh air. Other days were better – when I enjoyed an entire hour in the square.

When I was still on trial I received a present from the men on The Island. They put a few cents together and bought me a box of chocolates from the prison shop. The chocolates were old and pale but I enjoyed every one because the men sent them with many good wishes and much effort. Jama gave a Parker pen to my son Timol with his name engraved on it. That pen was very special. It was his first pen and he was only four.

For me, the end of my six–month sentence is within sight but many are not so lucky. Days go by slowly. I am far removed from the rest of my community. I tried to visit the group on The Island – without success.

Out of the blue one day, Amos Lengisi suggested that I undergo circumcision, although I do not remember telling him that I was uncircumcised. He mentioned that one of the PAC prisoners was an *ingcibi* (initiator) and could perform the ritual. After a young African male is circumcised, his family, relevant community structures and political organizations are notified, informing them that he is now a man. It was astounding to find out that such secret and sensitive ceremonies happened on the Island but circumcision was not part of my plan at that stage. My sentence was very short so I preferred to wait and take part outside prison walls. MK soldiers did not classify their members in terms of tradition or custom anyway. Lengisi accepted my decision and did not force the issue. Someone mentioned later that circumcisions took place in unidentified prison cells, using bandages and medicines stolen from the hospital. This could be a dangerous medical risk and carried the added risk of revealing this very secret ritual to white warders or men who were not yet circumcised.

Outside the prison, my family, lawyers and the ANC in Paarl organized a big event in celebration of my 27th birthday. Reverend Hunter of the Church of England and Reverend V.V. Mtini of the National Baptist Church defied the 'state of emergency' ban on political gatherings and held a party at St. Bernard Mizeki Anglican Church in Mbekweni. I could obviously not attend and did not bother asking for the impossible. Someone baked a birthday cake decorated in ANC colours. The event provided our grateful community with the opportunity of getting together.

During my imprisonment, I completed Grade 12 and then enrolled for a BA at UNISA (University of South Africa) in 1988. I was released from prison in 1990 during my second year of study.

CHAPTER 12

Unbanning of the ANC

For many South African citizens, the unbanning of the ANC was the greatest event of all. On the 2nd of February 1990 we heard F.W. de Klerk making the announcement on television. Initially, some of us did not understand what he meant because we were not familiar with the term he used; "rescinded" – so I looked it up in a dictionary. Mad with excitement, we raised a big ANC flag and *toyi–toyied* around the prison chanting slogans. Robben Island looked just like a tiny, liberated country that day. Joy shone from our faces and morale was very high. For the first time we cherished real hope. Prisoners began shouting *"Kuyahanjwa!"* ("We are going!")

Our excitement came to an abrupt halt after Nelson Mandela's release from Victor Verster Prison on the 11th of February 1990. Everyone became very angry. ANC communiqué, and the delegation from Robben Island who visited Nelson Mandela, assured us that he would be the last prisoner to be released, yet the opposite happened. We felt betrayed and very bitter.

The world celebrated his release with joy, but inside the prison things were a little different. Concerned about our plight and dreadfully confused, we completely misunderstood the situation. Everyone began having doubts and tried analyzing the situation, many saying that all eyes were fixed firmly on Nelson Mandela at that moment so the rest of us would simply be forgotten! We initiated another hunger strike, demanding our release. Among the prisoners were a few medical doctors. Dr. Ramlakan and Sibongiseni Dhlomo gave advice as to which men were fit to participate. They told us how to fast and listed things that could impact negatively on our health.

Mandela sent a delegation of lawyers, Pius Langa, Bulelani Ngcuka and others, asking us to call off the strike. Emotions ran very high as the men angrily expressed their dissatisfaction. Although hungry and weak, Sihle Mbongwa painfully translated from English into IsiZulu so everybody understood exactly what the lawyers were saying. (This was his specialty. In exile, Sihle translated whenever ANC leaders visited the camps). The lawyers carefully explained Mandela's position – and that of the ANC. We posed certain questions, which the delegation answered one by one. They informed us that prisoners would be released in phases. This finally convinced us so we called off the hunger strike, which, if I remember correctly, was in its ninth day. Thanks to Nelson Mandela and the maturity, articulation and negotiation skills of his lawyers, serious divisions among comrades were avoided. After this, some of the men began preparing for the day of their release.

Prison authorities were very pleased when the strike ended, even serving good meals, with dessert, prepared in the main kitchen. All prisoners received this special treatment – while it lasted. Normally only 'A Group' prisoners qualified. After the incident, officials relaxed a number of stringent rules.

We watched Britain welcoming Nelson Mandela at Wembley Stadium in London, mirroring the crowd's ebullient excitement. I cannot adequately express how we felt when Tracy Chapman and all the others lifted their voices to highlight our plight. Red Cross International, The International Defence Aid Fund, Amnesty International, Anti–Apartheid Movement, Lawyers for Human Rights, churches, other organizations and individuals in our country (and throughout the world) exerted pressure on South African authorities. We felt their presence, though separated by oceans and mountains. Their combined voices, prayers and lamentations helped tremendously in obtaining our release from prison and we are deeply grateful.

CHAPTER 13

Free at Last

It was wonderful to be among the first group of prisoners released on 3ʳᵈ September 1990 along with Lassy Chiwayo (the former MEC for Sports and Culture in Mpumalanga), Ntsikelelo Qaku from Queenstown, Sipho Nodlawu and many others. The authorities notified our families by telegram.

Jama's father with the telegram informing him of his release.

The provincial leadership of the Western Cape ANC received us at Cowley House, a place where families from distant places gathered and slept over when visiting prisoners on Robben Island. Ex–prisoners stayed there as well, awaiting travel arrangements. Today the building is almost forgotten, yet it should have been declared a museum as well. It is my belief that Robben Island and Cowley House are intertwined and inseparable.

I spoke on behalf of our group – the ANC in Prison – expressing how we felt about the process of releasing prisoners and the route taken by the ANC and Botha regime in securing our freedom. Trevor Manuel spoke with great maturity and passion on behalf of the ANC. No one knew whether our release was a direct result of discussions between the ANC and government or a conciliatory gesture to the international community.

That night I stayed at Gary Kruser's parents' place. The following day a busload of people from Paarl escorted me to Mbekweni, singing and chanting slogans. Having been in prison for almost six years, I honestly did not know how to react. One thing became clear; they had very high expectations. The organizers sat me down on the bonnet of a car and drove me through the township to the community hall. Barely able to contain myself, and still wearing the grey suit given to me on the day of my release, I took the platform but would be lying if I claimed to remember my speech that day. I was on top of the world.

Concerns emerged from other activists about local leadership. It became clear that the community wanted me to take on the role, automatically assuming the time spent in exile and prison better qualified me for the task. However, I still faced the circumcision issue. At one stage someone in the crowd mentioned that 'a boy' could not be allowed to lead them. I needed to be circumcised first. Whenever I raised a political issue, circumcision resurfaced somewhere within the discussion. No one seemed to care whether or not I had the financial means to undergo the ritual. In a nutshell; I won the political battle but not the cultural one. This hurt, yet I understood the cultural dynamics. The community put on the pressure and I struggled to find enough money to pay for my 'rite of passage'. Finally, I received a cheque from the International Defence Aid Fund. Mthetheleli and I took some of this money and left for the Transkei, undergoing all the necessary rituals. The practice always took place out in the veld, far from other people, especially women and uncircumcised boys.

After the initiation ceremony Mthetheleli and I did not put ourselves forward for leadership positions but offered to assist the ANC in whatever area they needed instead, indicating that the men who led the struggle while we were in prison should continue to do so. Being unemployed, we volunteered our services to the provincial executive as bodyguards, prior to being integrated into the new government system. My job included protecting the ANC leaders.

After my release from prison in 1990 I experienced both joy and, at the same time, concern about the uncertainty of my future. Accommodation and employment were high on my list of priorities. Education featured on the list as well. However, I told myself that all these issues would be attended to as soon as I was settled. At first I did not know how to react or behave when people from my township hailed me as a hero. Their accolades were too much to handle and exerted an incredible amount of pressure on me. People saw me as some sort of idol and I was constantly on guard not to fail them, particularly the youth. Both young and old wanted to chat about how I defied the magistrate by chanting ANC slogans in court or the courage and determination I showed during the trial. Some confessed to attending the trial merely out of curiosity. They wanted to see what a freedom fighter looked like, having heard propaganda from the apartheid regime that 'terrorists' were merciless people with no regard for human lives. I had to be extremely cautious of what I said to people and extra careful how I conducted my social life. I found myself having to live for others, not for myself. This was a big challenge and I was not prepared for it, never having received any counselling after I left prison. In fact, I never saw the necessity for undergoing counselling at that time, although I realize now that this was shortsightedness on my part.

My parents, sisters and brothers did not pressurize me at all, to either earn a living or become involved in an intimate relationship. I struggled with the latter at first. Although confident about a number of things, proposing to a girl was not one of them. In time, I gained confidence and had no problems approaching the fairer sex. I depended largely on my family for food and pocket money. Now and again temporary relief arrived in the form of funds from the ANC, who paid me for VIP protection operations. This amounted to between R50 and R100 a day and it made a huge difference. I knew and understood that the ANC would not be able to employ all activists but had obvious expectations of being employed full–time by the ANC.

At home, I had no accommodation of my own but shared an informal house in a back yard with my brothers, Zamile and Nomshayi. There was no privacy. My friends assisted me with regard to alternative accommodation but I had to move from place to place, depending on the availability of accommodation. I stayed with Thembekile and Nomfuneko Mangena for a while and had my own room, which I enjoyed very much. I also shared accommodation with John Mangena, a friend of mine. Whenever he was away, which was quite often, I had his room all to myself. This really was a relief.

My family is very large and it was depressing to see my sisters and their children sleeping on the floor because the house was too small. It was only a three–roomed house consisting of one bedroom, a kitchen, and a lounge. They had no mattresses but laid blankets on the cement floors. I felt really awful because I did not have any means of remedying the situation and this added to my stress level. I had to find work. Eventually I was employed as a Literacy Programme Coordinator. By then I was involved in a relationship with my current wife, Asanda, who was studying at Peninsula Technikon at the time. She offered her overwhelming support and helped to stabilize me. I stopped moving from place to place and stayed with her nearly every day. We eventually rented a flat in Cape Town. I married Asanda in 2002. She has stood by my side through the most difficult times of my life and her motivation and understanding are indispensable factors that helped to solidify our relationship.

My first wife is Yolisa Ngeva. We married in 1996, two years after she gave birth to my son Thando (in 1994). We were not ready and both rushed into the decision. Our daughter Ako was born four years later (in 1998) but our marriage only lasted for two years.

Jama and his wife, Asanda.

Jama's son Thando, at the age of 5 years, exchanging a few words of wisdom with Nelson Mandela.

Jama's daughter, Ako.

The ANC afforded me the opportunity of travelling to Sweden in January 1991 with comrades from other provinces, invited by the SAP (Swedish Social Democratic Party). Arriving virtually fresh from prison, this country played a significant role in my healing process. We went to study the people and trade unionism and share our experiences in South Africa. We spent our first night at the superb Kom Hotel in Stockholm, experiencing truly excellent service and staff – our first taste of what was still to come. We met with Billy Modise, the ANC's Chief representative at that time, and then went to see William Masango – whom I last met in Angola back in 1983. Here, we experienced a similar *umphando* (digging) routine to the one in Zambia: choosing secondhand clothes – this time from a small warehouse in Stockholm. Solidarity movements donated the clothes. Afterwards, we attended lessons at Brunnsvik Folk School, learning about the various Swedish political parties and trade unions and how to conduct study circles. Henry Blid facilitated the classes and did an exceptional job.

Reflecting on our situation in South Africa, we struggled to comprehend the fact that Sweden has a history of few labour strikes. Apparently this was the result of close working relationships between government and labour movements but we expressed fears that labour movements could easily be manipulated under those circumstances. They responded by saying that, although the various parties disagreed on certain matters, Swedish labour movements strive to forge unity between themselves and the ruling party. More importantly, they do everything possible to solve issues amicably. The absence of the death penalty in Sweden struck us as well. Surprisingly, the rate of crime at that time stayed below two percent, probably because the country was not engaged in any wars and they only gave passage to certain countries. In addition to this, Swedes did not stop inculcating citizens with the importance of personal responsibility. I experienced this for myself during a shopping expedition. Nobody policed the customers. Buying the paper was an education too. One simply helped oneself from a pile of newspapers on the pavement outside the shop and left the money to pay for it. I found it extremely difficult to accept. If one moved these businesses to South Africa, I guarantee that the shelves would be empty by the end of the day. We are, by no stretch of the imagination, even close to that kind of culture. With regards to changed mindsets, the challenge seems impossible to achieve in South Africa, at least for now. Our history of poverty truly left a devastating effect.

Our visit to Sweden not only benefited the Swedish people who heard about our experiences, but we gained insights into events that took place in our country as well. For instance, Minister Stella Sigcawu (the former Prime Minister of Transkei) told me that the coup staged by General Bantu Holomisa was a planned event in conjunction with the ANC. I am still unsure whether this is fact or not.

We made many friends in Sweden; including refugees from as far away as the Middle East. Kerstin Ahlberg accepted us as brothers and sisters, going the extra mile to ensure that our stay in Brunnsvik would be as comfortable as possible and always making her home available for socializing.

Prior to flying to Gotland we were welcomed by International Secretary Mr. Conny Frederickson as well as Malin Olsson, International Secretary for the Social Democratic Workers' Party. Citizens on the island of Gotland welcomed Masepeke Mapule and I – we soon fell in love with the place – although I entertained serious reservations at first because of my experiences on Robben Island, psychologically equating one island with the other. Gotland is a tourist attraction with many historical buildings and one of the loveliest places to visit in Sweden.

I stayed with Styles Mazibuko, a former member of uMkhonto weSizwe, and his Swedish wife Mygun. Styles lived in Sweden for many years and eventually took up citizenship. He opened my eyes regarding MK activities in camps during the sixties. I related to certain things he mentioned, such as the difficulties of life in exile. He and his wife condemned South Africa's apartheid regime. They helped tremendously in giving me an understanding of the Swedish people. Mygun gave me all the necessary support whenever I spoke to various groups of people and worked tirelessly to make sure we attended every scheduled meeting. She called me her son and I, in turn, called her mother. Besides the Mazibuko family, others warmly received us into their homes as well, including Tommy Gardell, one of the leaders of the ILO (International Labour Organization) trade union.

Jama in Gotland, standing and sharing his experiences with Union members.

Members of the Social Democratic Party accompanied us to meetings. I spoke about my experiences and my country, putting certain issues into the right perspective, particularly 'black on black' violence as the Swedes repeatedly brought up the subject. Evalena our interpreter helped with audiences who had difficulty understanding English.

We spoke to pupils at Savë High School and Steynska Primary School, telling them about South Africa and our struggle against oppression. Many students displayed great ignorance, believing that we lived in a largely unpopulated country with wild animals occupying the greater part. After our talks, people agreed that they had a role to play as well, not only during the apartheid era but, equally, once we attained freedom. We addressed a few churches and, at one of them, the ISAK (Isolate South Africa Group) asked us to try and persuade a certain church in the area to accept refugees about to be thrown out due to the unsympathetic attitudes of the congregation. We held a fruitful session at a Baptist Church. They promised to keep us in their prayers, showing great concern about South Africa and raising fears that we might be arrested or killed on returning home. During meetings and discussions, a number of people confessed to a previous misunderstanding of South African politics and thanked us for our input. After returning home, I received letters from quite a few of them.

I promised myself to return one day and thank the people of Sweden – and Gotland in particular. Due to financial limitations, the dream is not yet a reality but this does not mean my promise will never be fulfilled. If not during my lifetime, the honour will be left to one of my descendants or comrades. The Swedish SAP and ABF (*Arbetarnas Bildnings Forbund* – Worker's Educative Association) and the ANC gave us an opportunity of a lifetime. The words of wisdom we received and the realization that, somewhere in the world, people really care means a great deal to us. Their genuine concern for my safety made me a stronger person at that stage because I could not predict what the future would hold.

In 1991, the University of Stellenbosch invited Nelson Mandela to speak. I returned home and continued with my work, becoming one of the proud and determined team of bodyguards who escorted him to Stellenbosch, willingly putting my life at risk. Concerns about the possibility of an assassination attempt by white radicals kept us alert at all times. Arriving at the hall, we noticed a group of white Afrikaner students in the audience holding the old South African flag. Completely ungovernable, they booed Mandela and made a lot of noise. Trevor Manuel instructed us to remove them from the hall. In the process they vehemently resisted but we eventually managed to force them outside. Police and security forces arrived but Jeremy Veary (who was in charge of the operation) drew an imaginary line on the ground threatening that, if the police crossed it, we would fire. Fortunately no one forced the issue and the drama ended peacefully. Mandela continued his speech as though nothing had happened.

Within that same year I attended an ANC conference in Durban, part of a protection unit escorting buses taking delegates from Cape Town to Durban. Mandela was due to deliver a speech at a rally in the stadium after the conference. Early that morning his wife Winnie came to ask for a copy of the speech in her husband's briefcase. No one knew where the briefcase was. Furious, Mandela demanded that someone find it immediately. Sometime later, Andrew 'Madiba' Khumalo, the guard responsible for Nelson that day remembered that the briefcase was in the boot of Mandela's car, a BMW. The driver was on his way back to Johannesburg. Fortunately the car had a cell phone so he immediately turned around and drove back to Durban. Without technology the entire event would have been a disaster – for all of us.

At the conference we were disappointed when Oliver Tambo announced that he would not be standing for the ANC Presidency. His health had deteriorated after suffering a stroke. Chris Hani declined the nomination to stand in and Nelson Mandela was elected.

I counted it a great honour to take command of Nelson Mandela's pre–election campaign visit to Paarl. The event took place in February 1994 as a means of winning the district over to the ANC. Nelson visited Victor Verster prison first and then addressed the crowds at a packed Dal Josafat stadium. On our way to the stadium we heard shots from a nearby vineyard. I warned Vusi Tiyo (currently a commander in the National Protection Services – SAPS) over the two–way radio. Vusi drove Dr. Allan Boesak's car but reacted before he received my message. He provided cover until we left the danger area, displaying great skill. I appreciated him taking the initiative. We did not stop the convoy but asked the police to investigate instead.

Bodyguards provided protection without pay, driven by passion and commitment and often arriving at work very early and leaving very late. At times, many of us functioned on no more than three or four hours sleep.

During the same period, Rev. Mtini from the Baptist church and I drove to Paarl to tell Major Le Roux that I was alive and kicking. In detention, Le Roux once told me that if I refused to work for the police I would rot in jail. It was a great satisfaction to face the man responsible for taking me away from my family and putting me in prison.

I found it difficult to rest. The ANC youth kept nagging me to send them for military training so I got in touch with underground comrades to see what I could organize. At one stage I spoke to Welile 'Monwabisi' Salman at Mdantsane near East London in the Eastern Cape. He had been my military combat instructor at Caxito and was then recruiting and helping individuals to leave the country. I managed to organize for several Paarl and Cape Town youth to get to Botswana. Chris Hani operated underground at Enkululekweni in the Transkei and insisted that the youth be trained there first. At the time of our conversation I had a mini–bus full of recruits, all putting pressure on me to leave the country, and I had to organize accommodation for them as well. We had driven all the way from Paarl and were on our way to Bloemfontein station. I intended taking them to Botswana, no matter what. The question of funds rested squarely on my shoulders as my passengers all had empty pockets. Thankfully, Max Kweleta, Dicksen Teboho Phokeng and others helped to finance these trips.

The University of Venda hosted an MK conference in 1991. I attended with the Western Cape delegation, having flown from Cape Town to Johannesburg. Mini–buses took us to Venda from there.

Nelson Mandela, Chris Hani and General Bantu Holomisa (then the head of Transkei) spoke at the conference. We deliberated on a number of issues and certain positions were taken, the most critical issue being the integration of MK soldiers into the South African Defence Force (SADF). People expressed concerns about an MK/ SADF merger. Many felt that the process would not be integration but absorption. We were insufficiently prepared for the transition from a non–conventional army into a conventional one. Some of the recommendations highlighted the need to take homeland armies on board as well, particularly from the Transkei, and we stressed the need for SADF transformation. There was a call for cadres to be trained in preparation for their new roles. General Bantu Holomisa warned against unnecessary compromises from ANC leadership and looked directly at Nelson Mandela saying, "With due respect to you, Comrade Mandela, the ANC is compromising too much." We put forward ideas and discussed solutions before parting, with the understanding that all the issues would soon be addressed.

Today, viewing the Defence Force from a distance, my heart is filled with sorrow simply because the MK spent so much wasted time and effort in contributing towards building a future and bringing about a new dispensation. We did not know it at the time, but our efforts were undermined. Sadly, we experienced serious problems in the army during the infant stage of democracy. In all honesty, we failed to properly apply our minds and provide workable solutions.

In February 1995, ex–Robben Islanders came from all corners of South Africa for a reunion. Dr. Dhlomo, Sfiso Buthelezi and a few friends arrived from Cape Town to attend. We had all been in prison together. Having recently bought a house, I offered them accommodation for the night. We arrived home very late that night, utterly exhausted. I switched on the lights – and nothing happened. It was pitch dark. The electricity was off so we felt our way to the bedroom, but I forgot to inform my guests that I only had sponge mattresses with no bed bases. Dr. Dhlomo slept under protest that night but there was nowhere else he could go at that late hour. The next day I received a few irate phone calls from comrades complaining that I let the good doctor sleep on the floor. He never fails to remind me of it, every time we meet.

The next day we boarded the 'Outeniqua' and sailed out to the Island. It was wonderful to renew old acquaintances, although one thing did disturb me. Signs of frustration and dire poverty lined the faces of so many comrades. At the quarry, each man added a stone to build a monument, indicating his past presence as a prisoner on Robben Island. It is there to this day.

In prison, we had always been there for one another. Our sense of community disappeared after being released and many men had to fend for themselves. The ANC did not look closely enough at the plight of ex–political prisoners, former exiles and activists – the very people we should have been empowering and adequately equipping to transform our society. It is even worse for those who were trained to kill.

The last blow fell when we gathered at Peninsula Technikon in Bellville to elect a national structure of ex–political prisoners. We were sure that, by electing high profile people like Ahmed Kathrada (Chairperson of the committee), Tokyo Sexwale, Terror Lekota, Popo Molefe and others, the plight of many destitute comrades would be properly addressed. This proved to be a mistake. For the previous seven years the committee failed to convene on many occasions. Instead they were engaged in other activities that they probably deemed more important. Sadly none of them allowed other men, who had the time and the will, to take over this task.

CHAPTER 14

Disbanding uMkhonto WeSizwe

In 1993 the news of Chris Hani's death arrived when I attended a comrade's funeral at St. Francis Community Hall in Langa Township. Sindi Mbobo broke the news with tears in his eyes. The assassination had just been announced on the radio. Sindi's statement caught me by surprise. Any hope of Hani highlighting the plight of former MK soldiers came to an abrupt end.

Harry Gwala spoke after the shocking announcement saying, *"Inja izohlala iyinja noma ungayinqamula umsila."* ("A dog will remain a dog even if you cut its tail"), adding that whites would never change no matter what happened. While negotiations took place in Pretoria, the *boers* continued to kill our people. The atmosphere changed after that and uncontrollable crying erupted throughout the hall. David Dlali and Tony Yengeni organized a few of us to meet secretly at the FAWU (Food and Allied Worker's Union) offices in Gugulethu. They told us that the South African government had killed Chris Hani and we needed to retaliate. We welcomed their suggestion unanimously. Instructions were very clear; make the Western Cape ungovernable by conducting a series of coordinated attacks, targeting the military and police. David Dlali supplied grenades. Mthetheleli Titana and myself were to coordinate attacks in the Boland area.

ANC leaders called on everyone to calm down because of the imminent elections. The ANC won so we put an end to our plans. A

107

national call to surrender all weapons took place after they came into power. I gave my weapons to Allan Paulse who, in turn, handed them over to the police.

Chris Hani's funeral service was held at the First National Bank stadium in Johannesburg. Seeing the body of this great man in an open coffin moved everyone deeply, particularly Nelson Mandela and Oliver Tambo. A large number of jubilant exiled MK soldiers from as far away as Uganda came to pay their last respects. None of us thought these soldiers would ever be allowed to attend a function in South Africa and some had had no contact with their families for years.

Hani and Tambo spent a lot of time with the soldiers in exile and understood them better than any of the other leaders. During the process of negotiation with the South African government many soldiers were disgruntled because they felt as if Nelson Mandela had sold them out by begging for freedom. They no doubt wanted the ANC to continue with the armed struggle and overthrow the government. I remember one of Helen Suzman's questions at the Five Freedom Forum delegation. She asked whether the ANC had ever considered suspending the armed struggle. The question irritated Tambo and he answered that they did not have a history of violence. The South African government had forced them to take up arms. He cited examples of many peaceful deliberations in the past when the ANC negotiated with government, yet all their attempts failed, forcing the organization to take up arms. Tambo suggested other strategies to present to the government, including the release of all political prisoners. He added that South Africans in exile should all be allowed to return home.

The South African government refused to negotiate with people like Chris Hani, whom they believed was a Communist. As a result he was not part of the negotiating process. This angered the soldiers. They felt that the ANC compromised too much, almost to the point of selling out. The negotiation process came very close to creating serious division among ANC members.

On one occasion, while I was still in prison, Nelson Mandela addressed the soldiers in exile after his release and I gathered there was resistance within the ranks of the MK. They could not understand the necessity of negotiating with the enemy. We all had different opinions on the matter. I think Nelson Mandela must have realized that peaceful negotiation was the only way. He no doubt believed that the ANC could outclass the apartheid regime at the negotiation table, whereas an armed struggle would take time and lives would be lost in the process. In any event, more positives than negatives resulted from the process. It was the best decision particularly as Tambo, together with the ANC leadership, secured the conditions contained in the Harare Declaration during their deliberations in Zimbabwe. The document demanded the release of all political prisoners, the removal of the state of emergency, the reinstatement of banned political organizations and the return of exiles etc.

I was overwhelmed with excitement and nostalgia when we finally disbanded uMkhonto weSizwe at Orlando Stadium on 16 December 1993. I shall never forget this event and was so proud of wearing my MK combat uniform freely in my own country. I met up with a number of soldiers, some of whom I last saw in Angola. All of us fought to free our people from oppression. The military commands and drills brought back great memories. We may not have been paid for our services in money – but we were certainly rich in our souls. Ex–soldiers mingled together and shared great moments. It was indeed a fitting ending – the final page in our book. Soldiers marched past, saluting their leaders for the last time. Our leaders sat at the front of a stage draped in ANC colours. Nelson Mandela, our Commander–in–Chief, stood up to salute us. I saw Winnie Mandela in her MK military outfit among the ANC giants. She showed great respect for the occasion and unquestionable excitement. Many soldiers thought of her as a woman of substance and a symbol of resistance.

Thousands of people from SOWETO (South Western Township) celebrated the occasion as well. They came in droves and their presence made us proud. As always, our people stood fully behind us. Although exhilarating, one could not help noticing the reality of the situation. Difficulties confronted a large number of soldiers and were a common topic of conversation. So many unemployed comrades – yet they still expressed unwavering support for the organization that developed their mental capabilities and political understanding. Their sacrificial service received acknowledgement that day, irrespective of the derogatory labels many have since been given. They made sacrifices to reshape the history

Disbanding of uMkhonto weSizwe – Jama sharing a great moment with other soldiers.

of our country and no one can dispute that. Even so, many expressed concern that some of our leaders had abandoned us.

Afterward, David Moisi and I travelled back to Cape Town, still wearing our uniforms. At a garage in Kroonstad where we filled up with petrol, people demonstrated a sense of pride and cheered us on. We even took photos with the petrol attendants. When we arrived home the youth and women celebrated in jubilation, ululating and shouting, *"Viva Mkhonto!"* It felt good to be recognized as heroes by the people we fought to liberate.

I looked for Wyne Durr for some time after that, wanting to fulfill the promise made in prison. Out of the blue I spotted him in a grey Audi while driving past Klein Parys on my way to Paarl East and flagged him down. He was with a colleague and recognized me immediately. I thanked him profusely, took down his details and promised to contact him soon.

At that time, I was still a part–time, unpaid, volunteer bodyguard with the ANC, training to be a Literacy Coordinator for a non–governmental organization. When I saw Wyne again, he possessed no money, car or home and was divorced. The thing that frustrated him most was not getting custody of his sons, whom he loved dearly. Wyne longed to reconcile with his wife but told me other forces were at play so I assured him of my help and support. We went to the place where he lived and I battled to hold back my tears. The man had no decent bed to sleep on. I sat down on a plastic milk crate, wishing I had money to give him and blaming God for the pathetic state of my own finances. Wyne now lived with the poor white community in Paarl. For the first time in my life, I discovered that poverty was not confined to one particular race.

Later on, he phoned from a mental hospital at Stikland near Bellville and asked me to visit. I went with a friend of mine. It hurt to see him walking towards me, obviously mentally disturbed. I realized how his physical health had deteriorated as well. He kept reassuring me, saying his brain needed a rest and he had a lot of things on his mind. During the apartheid era, Wyne witnessed dreadful things done to black people – things he tried hard to forget. We both knew the difficulties one faced in coming to terms with things like this. He added that his supervisors had poisoned him for five to six years to make sure he stayed in hospital.

During that period his wife divorced him, without him being aware
of signing the papers. Wyne asked me to buy a birthday card for her. I
was more than happy to help and bought a cake, champagne and flowers
into the bargain. I presented the gifts on Wyne's behalf and wished her a
happy birthday. She was taken by surprise and accepted with visible
appreciation, writing a note to her ex–husband in return.

Wyne and I stayed in contact. In 2000 I introduced him to Ingunn
Sofie Aursnes who was in South Africa at that time. She helped him to
regain some of his strength. He tried very hard to find work after that
but has not yet succeeded and still suffers from depression. Through
Allan Paulse, Wyne assisted the government with sensitive issues such as
exposing and investigating gun smuggling and other criminal acts aimed
at undermining our democratic government. Allan was by then a lawyer
and the former Mayor of Paarl.

CHAPTER 15

South Africa's First Democratic Elections

We all dreamt of seeing a change in South Africa. Obviously, for that to happen, we expected the ANC to lead us to the final realization of our dream. They counted on both internal and external forces for the attainment of this vision – internal forces being the people of South Africa and external forces the international community – and deployed personnel to different places and institutions in order to adequately represent the ANC.

Some were sent to strategic positions. Others took the initiative and placed themselves in areas of national interest. I worked for an NGO organization called The Ecumenical Action Movement (TEAM). I was placed there through a programme facilitated by the World University Service (WUS), an organization responsible for funding projects and headed by Phumzile Mlambo–Ngcuka (Minister of Minerals and Energy at the time of writing). In addition to my responsibilities as a Literacy Programme Coordinator, I continued as a part–time ANC bodyguard.

Prior to the 1994 elections, the ANC sent a group of twenty men from different provinces to the USA for training in VIP protection. The American government provided our training. After I completed the course, the ANC's Department of Intelligence and Security (DIS) deployed me to head the security component of the IEC (Independent

Electoral Commission) in the Western Cape. I left TEAM to pay fulltime attention to my new and challenging responsibility.

DIS gave me a basic team of employees to work with and I recruited others whom I felt could add value to the unit. My first challenge involved working closely with Brigadier Muller from the South African Police and Captain Krause from the Parliament's VIP unit. We were responsible for setting up a security infrastructure for key IEC offices in the Western Cape area. Muller's involvement took place at a strategic level, while Krause took charge of operations. I interacted with both of them at the different levels. We discussed work–related issues such as operational planning and discipline. This was not an easy task, considering that we came from vastly different backgrounds. ANC agendas made them suspicious as well as the possible threat of a government takeover.

We visited police stations and spoke to senior personnel regarding back–up systems and the provision of personnel to work closely with ANC security in towns with IEC offices. We tackled obstacles such as racism and subtle resistance to change. Krause played a big role in alleviating his colleagues' fears and certainly did his part. Working together to make sure the elections would be free and fair was my primary concern. We also needed the SAP's full cooperation. When we did receive it, we placed security personnel in those offices. The ANC gave me lists of people in those particular areas to take on board. I met with the committees or individuals, told them the requirements and how sensitive the job was and emphasized the need for discipline to ensure that we protected the ANC's image. In places such as George, Beaufort West and Vredendaal, they raised concerns about allowing the police to work closely with us, in case they tried to sabotage the process. A few felt the police who massacred our people could not be the custodians of a democratic process.

These were some of the realities I was confronted with whilst trying to convince comrades that a winning solution meant working together. Krause and I made unbelievable progress. As a result, all the offices were staffed with both ANC and SAP personnel. I not only faced the problem of convincing my comrades to come on board but also of dealing with new problems emanating from working together – overall mistrust and racism and lack of co–operation from the SAP.

Cape Town and George proved to be the most problematic areas. I sent Babase Tiyo (currently a superintendent with the SAPS) to take control of the office in George after receiving reports of instability. I dealt personally with the Cape Town office. ANC personnel alleged that racism prevailed and the SAP had denied our patrol guards access to the police radio, reducing them to 'traditional watchmen with *knobkerries*' (The word refers to African fighting sticks with knobby heads but, in this instance, simply meant that the watchmen were expected to defend property without arms or ammunition). The radios belonged to the police yet we needed to overcome this technicality so we finally decided to allow both parties to use them. The SAP retained responsibility for their property.

Two policemen undermined our female comrades. During the night, they switched off the lights and tried to frighten them, pretending to be ghosts. I investigated the allegations, found them to be true and approached Muller and Krause, highlighting the seriousness with which I viewed the matter. I briefed the SAP and our personnel, underscoring zero tolerance when it came to that sort of behaviour. The culprits showed disrespect so I immediately discharged them and gave an order denying them access to the building. Informing Muller of my decision, I asked him to provide replacements and our work continued.

I need to acknowledge Mr Geldenhuys, known as J.J. at this point. An argument erupted with certain senior police detectives who visited our offices. J.J. asked them to leave their weapons with security, assuring them that they would be locked in a safe. They refused. J.J. gave them two choices – hand over the guns and gain access to the building or keep them and leave the premises.

It came to my attention that protesters planned a sit–in to disrupt IEC activities but I salvaged that situation by asking management to address their concerns. Fortunately, most of the groups included people who knew me and were eager to listen. A sensitive issue cropped up with regards to staff, including myself, who worked without receiving any form of remuneration. I held a series of meetings convincing my staff to have faith and confidence, and promising to look into the matter. I reminded them of our obligation from a political perspective. Many staff members in our security department had family commitments and other obligations. They agreed to wait – but not forever. I spoke to the IEC head office but their response was very slow so I asked Mr. Albert Beukes from the finance department to arrange an air ticket to Johannesburg for my deputy, Helena Small, and gave her instructions not to return to Cape Town until the matter was finally sorted out. She made a significant breakthrough and the staff soon received payment. That helped a great deal, as I could not honestly justify the lack of remuneration considering the diligence with which they rendered their services. ANC security personnel worked with unwavering commitment and exceptional dedication.

Head Office commended us for being the only office in the Western Cape in which IEC property was adequately protected. We returned all their vehicles intact as well as computers and other equipment, thanks to immense cooperation between the SAP, ANC and IEC personnel. SAP staff consistently carried out their tasks to an exceptional standard. We received incredible assistance from IEC management and staff. Through their extra effort and understanding, we protected property, lives and information.

Within the ANC personnel, a few outstanding individuals made us proud and I went to the extent of training them in VIP protection. Faizal Moosa, who trained with me in the USA, assisted. The exercise paid dividends later on when they were amalgamated into the government's National Protection Services.

DIS held a meeting sometime later at their office in Woodstock to choose people for integrating into new government structures. I represented my staff but, feeling strongly that such selections were a sensitive matter, asked that my personnel be allowed to attend in person. Contrary to the DIS's subsequent ruling, I brought them to the meeting and discovered many new faces among the potential candidates, including relatives and friends. This smacked of nepotism. The provincial head of the DIS reminded me of their decision not to allow my team to participate and asked them to leave. In addition to this, they excluded a number of former MK cadres who had provided protection to ANC leaders yet I could not think of a more ideal opportunity for taking them on board. Seeing no possible justification for any of this, I picked up my briefcase and left the room but my staff soon convinced me to return. The committee insisted that none of my staff would be integrated but after a struggle I won the battle.

Having been a victim of these very practices myself, I became convinced that certain people did not want us to climb the ladder of success and claim the fruits of our labour. No individual or group can claim sole right of ownership to the struggle. I had already been excluded from joining the Western Cape Department of Intelligence and Security Directorate simply because I raised concerns about unfair practices. Certain individual agendas differed dramatically from those of the ANC. My deployment to the IEC was obviously part of an exercise to marginalize me as well but I made the best of it, fully aware of the general confusion and lack of guidelines in the event of possible security incidents – yet doing everything in my power to ensure that the integrity of the ANC, my staff and myself remained intact.

During the second election in 1999 the NIA seconded me to the IEC in the capacity of Assistant Security Director for the Western Cape. At that time, Rev. Courtney Sampson headed the Western Cape branch. I rendered my services for a month, arriving with systems and measures for ensuring that every security arrangement would be put in place, concentrating more on physical security and relying on the NIA for other services. Sofie Inngun is a judge, so she came from Norway to assist in monitoring the elections. At management meetings she showed great concern about free and fair elections in South Africa and asked me, on numerous occasions, if townships were adequately taken care of. She went with me to these areas, complaining about the lack of adequate staff and fearing that, if nothing was done about it, certain parties could lose a number of votes – denying black people a say in the future government of their country. Her commitment deserves applause. I admired her keen interest and zeal in seeing to it that officials carried out the process correctly. She remarked on the highly visible problems of racism and poverty that confronted South Africa as well. Her selfless actions carried a clear message – South Africans needed to work hard and show their commitment to their country and its people.

Rev. Sampson and Luyudu Ntusi made my task far easier. I was working in an area familiar to me and I had plenty of experience in the field of security. I cannot overemphasize the pressures we experienced, caused by logistics and the IEC's inability to meet demand with supply. As a result, there were insufficient voting material and officials. This created security problems at the end of the day. Voters began forcing their way into small stations, especially in Khayelitsha. Inadequate communication forced me, on many occasions, to calm the crowds down. Occasionally, panicking officials called in the police, creating anger and bitterness among voters.

From that experience I learnt that organizing a national election is no simple task. All role players should have been involved from the beginning and plans prepared well in advance. Staff and voters ran all over the place, disorganized and directionless as though the elections came as a big surprise to everyone. Elections have an impact on our country in terms of security, due to the increased movement of people and traffic. We need to invest in our society by gradually transferring knowledge about election procedures, and the importance of voting, to ordinary South Africans. There are many ways this can be achieved, other than overloading citizens with a lot of material that often results in further confusion. The process of teaching people to vote responsibly should never be left to the last minute, but implemented regularly and constantly between elections.

CHAPTER 16

Violence in the Western Cape

A series of violent attacks in the Western Cape took place in 1999, causing panic among South African citizens and tourists. Shopping malls were bombed and this created uncertainty and pessimism. Security forces tried their best to apprehend the perpetrators. I worked for the NIA as a Security Advisor at the time. Achmad Cassiem and Jusuf Patel were alleged to have great influence on PAGAD (People against Gangsterism And Drugs), an organization suspected of carrying out such attacks. They belonged to an organization called 'Qibla'. Both were predominantly Moslem organizations. Patrick Ricketts told me that the ANC and the government were terribly disturbed about the spate of violence in the Western Cape so we needed to talk to these comrades on an unofficial level. Patrick and I had worked alongside these men during the apartheid years. We respected one another and had exchanged ideas although we came from different political organizations.

We arranged a meeting at Ansaf Mohamed's home in Ottery and deliberated on the matter. I voiced anger and disappointment that our own comrades were undermining the democratic government we had all voted into power. I accused them of trying to topple the very government we fought for and explained that they had no legitimate reason for taking up arms.

Achmad and Jusuf articulated their concerns but did not admit to being PAGAD members. However, they believed the government was corrupt, unable to fight crime and that their policies failed to address real issues, especially foreign policy. The welfare of comrades who sacrificed their lives for the attainment of freedom left much to be desired. The government had betrayed the nation. They cited examples in Islamic countries where former liberation fighters received discount tokens to use for public transport, housing, education and medical treatment and complained that intelligence structures were highly infiltrated and ineffective. Government excluded many people who could make a tremendous contribution.

Patrick and I agreed with them on some of these issues, having encountered similar problems during the integration phase. We too recognized the need for fast–track delivery. However, problems could never be solved through violence. Patrick promised to raise their issues with government. Everyone agreed that lines of communications needed to be opened and we encouraged them to take part in governing the country. In turn, Achmad and Jusuf undertook to try and persuade PAGAD to put their operations on hold and strive for possible solutions.

We gathered they had lost faith in the government and the manner in which it was running the country by failing to address important issues such as poverty. A highly principled person, Cassiem could be very controversial at times but, once he was convinced about a certain cause, he never gave up easily. Patel was more flexible and keen to solve problems rather than adding to the fire. It is my belief that, irrespective of the concerns politicians had about those men, they actively participated in bringing about the new dispensation and, as such, their welfare ought to have been addressed in the same manner as any other ex–combatant. All four of us were military men, South Africans concerned about the plight of our people. No one held a grudge and we aired our frustrations, understanding one another and speaking the same language. Not a stranger to these types of negotiations, I left fully convinced that we had achieved our objective. It came as no surprise when I learned about the subsidence of PAGAD activities sometime later. I was happy to see myself contributing positively in resolving a matter of national concern, although the results were not instant.

CHAPTER 17

Khumbula Healing Centre

The Khumbula Healing Centre started out as nothing more than an idea from as early as 1996, five years after Chris Hani, a member of the ANC National Executive Committee, visited the families of fallen comrades in the Western Cape. He promised to assist them by bringing back the remains of heroes and heroines who died outside South Africa.

Families of the affected persons put pressure on Hani to make such an undertaking. They wanted to lay their dead to rest in order to accept and come to terms with their death. In the process of waiting for this to happen, Hani was killed and nothing materialized. People who knew about the undertaking did not want to pursue the matter, as it was a sensitive issue that needed determination and strength to carry out. Some indicated that moral and cultural dynamics had the potential to create division within various organizations and might prick wounds even further. As a result, no proper structure was set up. The Truth and Reconciliation Commission was seen as a suitable vehicle for healing the nation's hurt. This inspired many activists in Paarl to engage in debate and discussion on the matter. Khumbula was formally launched on 16 December 1998. I was a founder member.

This non–governmental organization has five objectives; the exhumation of fallen fighters, the written recording of our history, the erection of monuments, healing, and the development of women and youth. As far as the first objective is concerned, a number of comrades who died outside the country are still buried outside our borders far from their families. Vivian Matthee died in the Lesotho Massacre of 1985. The South African Defence Force raided the tiny kingdom in pursuit of ANC 'terrorists' and killed a number of our comrades in Lesotho. Some are still buried there. One of the most moving moments I ever experienced was the exhumation of Vivian's remains in October 1999. We linked up with the (then) High Commissioner of South Africa in Lesotho, Mr. Alpheus Ndlovu. Vivian's family and our organization received a warm welcome. The foreign minister, Mr Thabane, and the people of Lesotho gave us their maximum cooperation. Mr Ndlovu was of great assistance in guiding us through the process and the necessary documentation that needed to be completed. As it was a dignified state occasion, I wrote a poem entitled 'Take Us Home' that Africa Hlapo read out to the audience.

TAKE US HOME

Forgotten sons and daughters cry out
Because their land is far away
Their cries carry pain and messages of sadness;
We were alive and heard our names called
To fight the oppressive regime
Yet when we were killed
They buried us in graves on foreign soil
Take us home!

We seldom hear our names called now
As we lie in deep graves far from home
There is no sky
There is no sea
There is no grass around us
All we see are walls of soil
We are left in the dustbins of history
Take us home!

We want to be buried and rest amongst the
Heroes and heroines of our struggle
Those who are fortunate to be remembered
We want to report to our forefathers in our own land
That families who gave so much for the country
Are deep in misery
We want to tell them; when all the praises are sung
We want to be there
When all the celebrations take place
We want to be there
Please, take us home!

We are tired, we are cold and lonely here
We have families in perpetual sadness
Because we are so far away and cannot be reached
We are fathers and mothers of children
Who need to communicate with us
Do not deny us the opportunity to be thanked by our loved ones
Who always kept us high in their spirits
Take us home!
Turn our graves into monuments of remembrance
Take care of our families whose hopes of survival once rested on us
Take us home!

Vivian's re–burial was well attended by the community. He received a fitting hero's burial. It was a sad yet joyful occasion because we were able to fulfill the wishes of families who never dreamed of being re–united with their loved ones.

On our first visit to Lesotho, Minister Thabane and Mr. Ndlovu shared a few of their experiences. The minister invited us for lunch at a hotel afterwards and mentioned that he ought to write some of them down. Sadly, the commissioner passed away in 2002, having never written his memoirs to the best of my knowledge. He and Mr. Ndlovu told us about a certain Mr. Smit from the South African army. This man saved Ndlovu's life during the apartheid days by giving him crucial information about a planned assassination. Mr. Thabane longed to meet him again to discover why Smit chose to save a 'terrorist's' life.

It struck me there and then that it was vitally important to preserve history by committing our experiences to paper as well. A really kind man, Mr Ndlovu always had the interests of the ANC at heart and not only assisted us with the exhumation of Matthee but of comrades Haas and Mfobo as well – whom our organization exhumed in Lesotho. They now lie at rest at Langa cemetery, close to their families. Autshumatu Investments sponsored flight tickets for the affected families. We made a worthwhile contribution. We buried Vivian at his hometown in a plot donated by the municipality. Khumbula negotiated for his plot and Anthony Sauls played a very important role. We hope that this land will one day become a heroes acre. Mthetheleli Titana's and Phumla Nkala's remains are interred here as well. They all took part in the struggle. Activists, former exiles and ex–political prisoners in Paarl will be buried on this land.

The writing of history by ordinary foot soldiers is the second objective of Khumbula. I am hoping that other comrades will follow my lead.

As a non–governmental organization, Khumbula does not have the funds to carry out our huge objectives. We are hoping that the small contributions we made to date will make a difference somehow, and we hope to do even more in the future.

CHAPTER 18

A Short Collection of my Poems

SUCH ARE THE MOMENTS

Such are the moments
When I lie in my bed
Thinking about all the wonderful hours we shared together
Experiencing the difficulties of an unforgiving earth
You suddenly appear in my dreams
Though I did not want you to
Such are the moments.

Such are the moments
When lovely memories became sad tales
I find myself helpless
Given the inescapable realities of life
I suffocate
When the things we treasure collapse
Such are the moments.

You left me in the cold to slowly die
You could have lifted a hand to help
I feel like a beheaded chicken struggling to live
Yet I cannot
You turned a cold shoulder to me
When I desperately needed the warm one
That was an unforgivable crime
Such are the moments.

Although I have fallen hard from the ladder of love
I will smoothly ascend the *HILLS OF HOPE*
Perhaps tomorrow will not be like today
Such are the moments.

LET ME SEE MY FATHER

Beaten, tortured in the enemy's dungeon
Degraded, dehumanized and left in an open field
To die
With no one to talk to
With no one to comfort.

My father's bullet–riddled body, cut into two halves
By people with no respect for human life
His body an instrument to scare those of similar conviction
And commitment
To fight injustice and liberate our people
Please, let me see my father.

I faced life and grew without him
People who claim to be Christians
Made me a fatherless child
Even so, please, let me see my father.

Let me bury his remains even if he is beyond recognition
Let me give him a decent burial
He was my father and remains my father.

I always respected him
No matter what you did to him
Please
Allow me to see my father
I do not ask you to give me money
I do not ask you to build me a house
I do not ask you to buy me a car
All I ask is to see my father
Let me see my father.

HELP ME, HELP ME

I was brought into this world like any other child –
Without my consultation, without my approval
Had I known that I would be an outcast
I would not have dared to come to this earth
Had I known that I would be eating from dustbins
And sleeping in the street on cold nights
Had I known that on hot days I would be standing there
begging for food
I would not have opted to be here
Help me, help me!

I am a child who is a victim of circumstance – a creation not to
my liking
My parents brought me into this earth and abandoned me
My age left me with no choice but to ask for help, to beg for food
My body is covered in scars from people who abuse me
No one protects me
I have nowhere to go
I am a child whose destiny has already been decided
by the unfriendly forces of this earth
Help me, help me!

I cry before sleep
I cry during sleep
I cry after sleep
I carry the punishment of a bigoted community
I am humiliated and suffer insults
When I ask for food in the streets
I am cursed and punished through no fault of my own
The pain I endure each day of my life
is something I never dreamt of experiencing
Help me, Help me!

If I deserve to die then I should not be here
If I am an unwanted child take me to a place of safety
Take me and give me the love I need
The caring, the warmth,
But don't abuse me
Help me, help me!

Give me the hug you would give to a child whom you love
Give me the love you would give to your own children
Take me to school as you would take your child
Take me for a drive as you do with your own
Help me, help me!

CHAPTER 19

Epilogue

Life is not always a bed of roses. Throughout my life I experienced difficult periods, yet shared a number of joyous and unforgettable moments with family, friends and comrades–in–arms, considering myself lucky to have survived and lived to talk about the road I travelled.

One of our expectations as soldiers during the time of the struggle was that the government would be overthrown through the use of weapons. We believed that, immediately after this was achieved, we would seize property and land and give them to our own people. We would choose the houses we wanted to occupy. Others expected to own farms, believing that the new government would distribute the country's resources. We were so sure that they would take care of the soldiers who fought for liberation as well. We would empower our people. We read about democracy and had no qualms in regarding its application. The ANC would govern the country and we never once doubted that the Freedom Charter would be implemented to its fullest. It was our bible and our daily bread.

We expected a hero's welcome for returning soldiers and imagined all the smiling and excited faces, families reuniting and old friendships re–activated. Sharing information and talking about our experiences, we intended to defend the gains of our revolution and were eager to sacrifice and die in the same manner as we did during exile.

All this was nothing more than soldier–talk – creative imagination to console and keep us determined to fight on. The peaceful transition came as a complete surprise. Certain conditions were stipulated and forwarded to the ANC, such as relinquishing violence as a means to attain our freedom. For many civilians, it was long overdue.

The route was not a short one as anticipated, but was far more complex than we imagined. The process had its casualties. Some of our own people turned to drugs, liquor and other forms of 'dealing' with stress, depression and frustration. Those who came out of exile included many who were imprisoned. They were not counselled or properly prepared to face the inevitable.

The reality of governance involved debates etc. Such proceedings can stretch over a long period and people grow impatient. The government is also constrained by the availability of resources. I believe this spilled over to the institutions that took us on board during the process of integration. Some of our people managed to contain or redirect their frustration, anger or depression. The unemployed suffered the same fate and, as a result, some communities are victims of this behaviour. It is not always easy to understand why some manage to overcome their problems and others do not. People are unique and often react differently. That is a fact of life and these are the realities our government and people are faced with. They still expect past values and principles to be upheld yet that appears to be something only a handful of men adhere to today. It has been a tough journey.

I find it a relief to voice my opinions and have derived great pleasure from assisting a number of comrades in one way or another.

Nothing is impossible, though some things take longer to achieve than others. I regard obstacles either as temporary setbacks or signs that give one direction. Signs to be observed and not ignored because they teach us something important or warn us about looming danger. When striving for 'the impossible', one needs faith and hope – indispensable intangibles – tools for one's development. If we lose these, we cease to be a person. I am stronger today, not *despite*, but *because* of all the trials.

I long for people to speak up instead of gathering in corners, doing nothing but complain. If we openly challenge wrongs and injustices, everyone would benefit and lead a better life. The government is not there to function in a vacuum. We should be watchdogs, ensuring that they have the best interests of those they profess to serve at heart. If one becomes aware of corruption or the misappropriation of resources, one should step forward. We fought for a democratic society and need to make sure we enjoy the fruits of our labour. Government officials are fallible human beings, just like the rest of us, and they will probably make some mistakes along the way. It is our job, as South African citizens, to ensure that their mistakes are minimal. We need platforms where people can safely voice their opinions. No one should be victimized or sidelined for having the country's interests at heart.

I see my role as that of uniting and helping to heal the wounds of my traumatized people and redirecting the energy of both blacks and whites. It is every citizen's responsibility to consider the future of our children, our country and particularly, of democracy. We need to stand together and use past experiences to prevent similar occurrences from happening in the future.

You may choose to call this indoctrination but what better time could there be to teach our citizens something we can all be proud of one day, irrespective of political affiliation? I love my country and want to contribute to its democratic development. It hurts me to realize that many white youths have never heard of an informal settlement, let alone know what they were like to live in. Many of them never set foot in a township because they are afraid of attack or reverse racism. The same goes for black children. Few of them try to understand what the white community is going through at the moment.

We need to find a practical way of merging those who live in villages, towns and cities – all our diverse people – into a solid block tied together by a sincere desire not to forget the past but to forgive one another. I realize that this is no easy task and carries risks, but it is certainly one worth taking. Surely it is better to step boldly forward in the pursuit of justice, peace and democracy than to shortsightedly stumble backwards because we are afraid of challenge, victimization or insult.

F.W. de Klerk and Nelson Mandela are symbols of the brave steps taken by men of stature to set aside their differences for the sake of their nation. They will not live forever. It is *our* duty to carry on their good work.

Jama's family:- Back from left : Lumka, Nomshayi, Jama, Zamile and Thembisa
Front from left : Fezeka, Oliver (Jama's father), Nobengazi (Jama's mother) and Thandiswa